HUGH O'BRIAN,
OR WHAT'S LEFT OF HIM

A Memoir

Hugh O'Brian
with Virginia O'Brian

Book Publishers Network
P.O. Box 2256
Bothell • WA • 98041
PH • 425-483-3040
www.bookpublishersnetwork.com

Copyright © 2014 by Hugh O'Brian and Virginia O'Brian

All rights reserved. No part of this book may be reproduced, stored in, or introduced into a retrieval system, or transmitted in any form, or by any means (electronic, mechanical, photocopying, recording, or otherwise) without the prior written permission of the publisher.

10 9 8 7 6 5 4 3 2 1

Printed in the United States of America

LCCN: 2014934098
ISBN: 978-1-940598-29-1 (hard cover)
ISBN: 978-1-940598-30-7 (perfect bound)

Editor: Barbara Kindness
Cover Designer: Laura Zugzda
Book Designer: Stephanie Martindale & Melissa Vail Coffman
Map of Africa © Kaarsten | Dreamstime.com

To Virginia—My Wife, My Life

Thank you for your love, support and encouragement. I am so very blessed to have "special" you come into my life. You ARE the most beautiful "LADY" inside and out that I have ever known.

CONTENTS

Foreword: by Debbie Reynolds	vii
Foreword: by Hugh Hefner	xiii
Introduction	xv
Acknowledgements	xvii
PART I: WHO IS HUGH O'BRIAN?	1
Chapter One: The Early Years	3
Chapter Two: From Lawnmower to Leading Man	21
PART II: GET ME HUGH O'BRIAN	33
Chapter Three: The Studio Days	35
Chapter Four: The First Adult Western	55
PART III: GET ME A HUGH O'BRIAN *TYPE*	73
Chapter Five: Broadway Lights	75
Chapter Six: On the Set	89
PART IV: GET ME A *YOUNG* HUGH O'BRIAN	109
Chapter Seven: The Legend Continues	111
Chapter Eight: Hugh O'Brian Youth Leadership (HOBY)	121
Chapter Nine: Messages from World Leaders	141
PART V: WHO IS HUGH O'BRIAN?	153
Chapter Ten: Staying Active	155
Chapter Eleven: Pitching for the Ninth Inning	175
Appendix A: Honorary Doctorates	185
Appendix B: Awards Received	186
Appendix C: Hugh O'Brian Credits - THEATRE	189
Appendix D: Hugh O'Brian Credits - MOTION PICTURES	190
Appendix E: Hugh O'Brian Credits - TELEVISION	192

FOREWORD

by Debbie Reynolds

I met Hugh when I was just starting out in the business as a teenager in Burbank, California. Never did I imagine back then that, decades later, I would consider him one of my dearest friends, but boy, am I glad I do. And even though a few years—give or take—have passed, I still see Hugh as the handsome and charming man who taught me many lessons that carried me through my career. One of the most valuable lessons, however, just so happened to correspond to the first time we met. It's how Hugh became known in the business as "King of the Kiss."

When I was a teenager, I had absolutely no experience with boys. I had always felt like a bit of an oddball. I was raised in a strict Nazarene household, and my family was very poor. I couldn't afford to buy the beautiful dresses and blouses that most girls wore to school, not to mention that I couldn't tell a tube of lipstick from a coloring marker. Don't even get me started on my hair!

My behavior didn't help much either. I was a troublemaker in school, climbing the flagpole and stealing the boys' shoes to throw them out the window. Nearly every day I found myself in the principal's office. I just loved to play jokes on people! And I loved to be a tomboy. I was even on the high school football team—I could throw better than my brother. He still hasn't forgiven me.

It wasn't until I discovered the thrill of the stage that I felt like I finally fit in. Acting was my salvation. At long last, a place where my practical jokes would earn me laughs instead of afterschool detention! When I got cast to play the female lead in *Singin' in the Rain*, everything seemed to fall into place. And then the unspeakable happened: I found out that I'd have to do an on-screen kiss with Gene Kelly.

Do you think I ever had dates, being the class clown that I was? The answer is never. I didn't go out with boys—I didn't even go to the prom! In addition, my conservative parents never taught me anything about the opposite sex. I'd never even held hands with a boy, let alone kiss one. Luckily for me, however, Hugh O'Brian entered the picture.

Back in those days, the movie studios would arrange dates between its stars for publicity purposes. They would send a car that would take the celebrity couple to a fancy restaurant or a movie première where photographers would be prepped and ready to go. Before we filmed *Singin' in the Rain*, the studio decided they would set me up on one of these dates.

Of course, my parents had to agree on the guy. He had to be a nice man, someone who might flirt, but would never try to kiss me or do anything nasty like that. So they set me up with Hugh O'Brian. And what a gorgeous man was he. I knew him not just from the pictures, but also from seeing him at all of the movie premières, and each time with some new, stunning woman on his arm.

Compared to Hugh's usual girls, I must have seemed like a kid sister to him. I think that's why we hit it off instantly. I sat and drank Coca-Cola and laughed the night away. Afterward, he took me back to my house where my father was undoubtedly

On a "publicity date" with Debbie Reynolds

waiting on the other side of the screen door with his baseball bat. Hugh walked me to the porch and, just as I was about to say goodbye, he said, "I'd like to kiss you goodnight."

My heart stopped. I said, "Oh, no. No, no, no. We're not going to do any of that funny stuff. This is just a publicity date and besides, I don't know how to kiss."

"Wouldn't you like to know how?" he asked. "Don't you have to kiss Gene Kelly in *Singin' in the Rain*?"

"Well, sort of," I said.

"If you're nervous about it," he said, "we can practice. I can show you how so you won't be afraid."

I always liked to rehearse and preferred to have a thorough understanding of what I was getting myself into, so Hugh's offer had a certain appeal. "Might as well," I answered.

Hugh is a tall man, whereas I was only five-foot-two, so he had me stand on the top step of my porch. "All right," he instructed, "now just relax. You can put your hands on my shoulders and just lean forward a little. Now close your eyes and I'll kiss you. You might not like it, but there'll be nothing that you dislike, I promise you. Who knows, maybe you'll even like it."

I said, "I doubt it, but go ahead." I practiced ballet and tap, so this was just one more thing to rehearse. Hugh started leaning forward and finally our lips met and he kissed me. I didn't feel anything. What was I supposed to feel? I didn't know. All I registered was that he had a nice, soft pair of lips. It was almost like kissing my cat or dog—just as soft and pleasant.

At last he pulled back and said, "See, that's kissing."

"Aw, that's nothing," I said. "I can do that."

So off he went and now I was an experienced woman—or so I thought. The day came when I had to do my kissing scene and yet I still found myself nervous about the big moment. Cameras surrounded us and Gene and I were posed in front of this gigantic billboard. The director called "action," and Gene came over to me, put his arms around me, and proceeded to stick his tongue down my throat.

I choked! I didn't know what was happening. This was certainly not like what I had rehearsed with Hugh!

I was so surprised that I gagged and ran off set, crying from embarrassment. It took a lot of convincing to get me back in front of the cameras. Now I find it amusing to watch that scene and see just how rigid Gene's mouth is in the take they used. I'm telling you, his lips didn't open even the slightest fraction of a millimeter! He certainly didn't try to choke me with his tongue after that first fiasco, anyway.

After that nightmarish experience, I thought back on my first kiss with Hugh and wondered if I could have prevented the experience with Gene from happening. You know what I realized? Hugh was a beautiful kisser, so soft and gentle, and because of that I thought that everything about men would be soft, sweet, and lovely. Sadly, that's not the truth! I just had to find out the hard way.

Now Hugh invites me to parties just so I can tell the story of how Gene Kelly stuck his tongue down my throat. I've kissed many men both onscreen and off since Hugh and Gene, but somehow those two remain my most memorable. Hugh O'Brian really is the "King of Kissers."

FOREWORD

by Hugh Hefner

I certainly knew Hugh O'Brian from his role as Wyatt Earp. He is one of the biggest television stars of all time.

Back in the 1960s, many people thought the two of us looked very much alike. I was once on a flight between Chicago and Los Angeles when a very attractive blonde approached me, gave me a beautiful smile, and engaged me in conversation. The answers I gave her must have been confusing, because she thought I was Hugh O'Brian and not Hugh Hefner. She even asked at one point, "You *are* Hugh, aren't you?" Of course I said yes! I don't know if she ever figured out that she was talking to a different Hugh from the one she had in mind.

The two Hughs—O'Brian and Hefner

I never took advantage of the strong resemblance between us, but I've got a feeling Hugh did!

In 1967, Hugh was starring in *Cactus Flower* which, after its eight-month run on Broadway, agreed to do it for several weeks in other cities. It sold out in Chicago where it ran an extra six months. He called to find out if there might be room at the Mansion so he could stay there during the run of the show. The Mansion had seven bedrooms, and celebrities typically stayed there while visiting Chicago, so there was certainly room for Hugh O'Brian. I always enjoyed Hugh's company.

Hugh is a good guy, and I am happy that our friendship has lasted this long. He and his lovely wife, Virginia, are regular Sunday night guests at my Mansion here in Los Angeles, and I'm always happy to see him and reminisce. I especially admire what he has accomplished with the Hugh O'Brian Youth Leadership (HOBY) program—he put his celebrity to very good use by helping so many tens of thousands of young people. In fact, Hugh had just returned from his visit with Albert Schweitzer when he was starring in *Cactus Flower*, and he did much of the work to establish HOBY from his room in the Chicago Playboy Mansion.

Our friendship is so deep that when I announced not long ago that I was planning on getting married Hugh sent me a note and offered to serve as a groomsman. The wedding was to be very small, and the only groomsmen were to be my two sons, so I regretfully declined Hugh's kind gesture. However, I certainly appreciated that token of our friendship.

Hugh O'Brian has had a long and wonderful career, and his HOBY program has motivated over 700,000 young lives. It is a remarkable accomplishment and he deserves a great deal of credit for it. Yes, he's a good guy and he's done good work and he's a good friend. It's a friendship that has lasted all these years, and friendships don't always last. So I'm happy that we're still in each other's lives after all this time.

INTRODUCTION

I've lived a very broad, eventful, and exciting life that has rewarded me tremendously. I've faced life not by asking "Why" but by asking "Why not?" Every step of the way, I've tackled—and continue to tackle—my adventures head-on. To me, living a good life is about having great curiosity about everything and the tenacity to go after what you want, while helping people along the way get what *they* want.

When I look back on my life's eventful journey, I divide the aspects of my life into five stages, which I call The Five Stages of Man. Or the Five Stages of Hugh, anyway. These are the inevitable phases of life that each and every one of us goes through. It doesn't matter how successful you have been or how wealthy you are…we all go through the same five stages of life.

The first stage, from birth until about age twenty-five or so, is the stage where others ask, "Who are you?" In my life, the question was: "Who is Hugh O'Brian?" This is the formative stage where you try to figure out what you want your life to look like.

In the second stage, people would say "Get me Hugh O'Brian." This is from about age twenty-six to forty. You've now begun to accomplish greater skill in your field, and people want you and pay you very well for what you do. Your focus is on how to get to the top of your game.

In the third stage, ages forty to fifty, those same people who hired you now say, "Get me a Hugh O'Brian type," because they don't want to pay you a high salary anymore. They want somebody who's like you, but new in the business, and who can be paid at a beginning salary level.

In the fourth stage, when you are in your fifties and sixties, people say, "Get me a young Hugh O'Brian." You're past your prime, but still well-respected in your business.

Then, in the final stage, just before you "bail out," the question again is, "Who is Hugh O'Brian?" In this fifth stage, what you've accomplished in the first four stages doesn't matter. You have no control over how other people perceive the work that you've done. You also have no control over when you exit that final stage and where you go when you do. It doesn't matter how important you were or how much money you have made. **You cannot buy forever**.

It's what you do—and how *well* you do those things—between stage one and five that counts.

This is the story of my life as Hugh O'Brian. Marine Drill Sergeant, athlete, lover, fighter, actor, philanthropist, brother, husband—and everything in between.

ACKNOWLEDGEMENTS

I have many people to thank for their support, encouragement, and various contributions that have made this book possible. From research, writing, editing, compiling photographs, or just plain being alongside me in love and friendship, I am very grateful to the following:

Sharon Crompton – Research/Photo Collections

Steve Dixon – Organizing, photo scanning & editing

David Glover – Research and website

Sheryn Hara and her associates at Book Publishers Network – For making sure the book was a quality product that readers would enjoy

Hugh Hefner – For your wonderful friendship and generosity

Don Krampe – My brother, and Jean, my sister-in-law, for your love and support

Michael Levin and staff – For getting my stories told

Stan Moger – For helping me with facts about *The Life and Legend of Wyatt Earp* and for sealing the deal to get the reruns back on TV

Ed Nixon – My friend, for introducing me to Sheryn Hara, publisher, and for your constant encouraging words

Pierre O'Rourke – Initial inspiration and research

Debbie Reynolds – For continuing love and support throughout my life

José Rivera – Thank you for helping me travel with the book upstairs, downstairs, then upstairs again, to the airport, and looking for the book

Tuan Van de Bui (a.k.a. St. Tuan) – For your beautiful photography and your special friendship over the years

PART I

WHO IS HUGH O'BRIAN?

Sgt. Hugh Krampe (O'Brian), USMC, Drill Instructor

Chapter One

The Early Years

I was born Hugh Charles Krampe in Rochester, New York, on April 19, 1925...or, as I like to put it, I was blasted out of a mountain. My dad, whom I was named after, was a model of the best traits of the men of his generation: self-reliant, tough, disciplined, motivated, and extremely upwardly mobile. From my first breath, as a member of the Krampe family, I saw firsthand what it means to take advantage of the great opportunities our country has to offer.

But my dad wasn't necessarily prepared for how quickly I learned.

When I was about four years old, our family moved to Chicago. We spent the first five weeks living in the Stevens Hotel on Lake Shore Drive. There was a candy store in the lobby, and every morning, if I had been a good boy, my dad would give me a couple of pennies so I could go down there and buy myself "jawbreakers" at a penny apiece.

One day, I guess I had misbehaved—I can't remember how, but I do remember the upshot: I didn't get my pennies.

"Never do that again," my dad told me. "You're not going to get your allowance today."

And he went off to work, leaving me feeling pretty sorry for myself. After pouting awhile, I took the elevator down to the lobby and wandered outside to the front of the hotel. There, on the corner, was this man with a large bag slung over his shoulder. It was stuffed with these flimsy things that didn't mean much to me at the time, though I would later learn that they were that day's newspaper, *The Chicago Tribune*. He was calling out over the bustle of traffic and pedestrians on Lake Shore Drive at morning rush hour, "Paper! Paper! Get yer paper!"

As I watched, passerby after passerby paused to hand the man coins in exchange for a newspaper. I thought to myself, *Boy, I know where there are a lot of those!*

So, I ran upstairs and got my Little Red Wagon that I had gotten for Christmas, and I went down to the hotel basement where there was a huge pile of what turned out to be old newspapers. I stacked my wagon high with them and dragged it out to the corner. I stood about twenty feet from the newspaper man and started mimicking him.

"Paper. Get yer paper!"

Pretty soon, men in suits and ladies in high heels started noticing me. Smiling, they'd stop to ruffle my hair, and quite often, they'd offer me a nickel or a dime for one of my papers. But I wasn't interested in those silver coins. I wanted the copper ones I could exchange for jawbreakers. So, I'd tell them, "Copper, please!" And I'd earn my pennies.

I did very well that day and I had to refill my wagon a couple of times. The next day I went back again. But by that time, the newspaper man had started to get ticked. I guess he was worried I was taking some of his business, so he went into the hotel and complained to the manager.

When my dad got home from work, the manager told him, "Mr. Krampe, I'm afraid we've got a little problem. Our newspaper man out front is upset that your son is trying to sell papers."

"What?" My dad had no idea what he was talking about.

"Yeah," the manager said. "Go out there. You'll see him."

My dad went out front, and there I was with my wagon full of the old papers. He grabbed me by the ear and yanked me upstairs to our apartment. He put me over his knee to spank me—but as soon as he did, a shower of coins poured out of my pockets.

"Hugh, don't spank the kid," my mother said. "He made more money than you did today."

And that's how things were at our home. My father was a strong disciplinarian, but my mother was part Irish and sure knew how to keep him in line!

My mother, Edith Krampe—born Edith Marks in Louisville, Kentucky—was a beautiful woman; a very loving, very generous, and very savvy lady. She was a true advocate. The first play that I did at the Lobero Theater in Santa Barbara, my mother stood out at the front of the theater and sold tickets. My dear mother passed away at a young age before she could see me on television as Wyatt Earp. She loved to play the piano, and whenever guests came to our home, they would ask her to play. My mother also loved her Manhattans, and after the second Manhattan, she would climb on top of the piano and dance. The complete opposite of my dad, my mother was a fun, very outgoing lady.

My parents had an enviable relationship that I could only dream of enjoying someday. I think they got along so well because they were polar opposites. Like any other couple, they had their occasional spats, but either my mother won or my father wisely walked away. They told me a story of how they'd separated for a couple of years before I was born, but then reunited and decided to stay together for good. To celebrate their reunion, they took a trip to Florida, where I was conceived at "The Breakers," the famous Palm Beach resort hotel.

My brother, Don, now also a retired Marine, came along four years later. We got along extremely well because he was my kid brother. When we were younger, I was often concerned about him because a few of his classmates frequently beat him up. I taught Don quite a few ways to defend himself. When he was old enough, he enlisted in the Marine Corps and served in Korea. Don is a wonderful man with great kids and a terrific wife, Jean. Professionally, he was the head of a local YMCA for many years, and has spent the last twenty-five happy years in Southern California with his family.

My dad was a very ambitious man so my life on the move started very early on. We moved quite often when I was young—from Rochester, New York, to Garden City, Long Island, to Grand Haven, Michigan, to Lancaster, Pennsylvania, and finally to Wilmette, Illinois, where Dad bought a beautiful home and we finally settled down. Dad was a key executive for a company that manufactured insulation and linoleum called Armstrong Cork Co. They're now Armstrong World and the biggest manufacturer of linoleum floors. When dad was transferred to Chicago in 1930, he was in charge of the Midwest, but also of overseeing everything west of the Mississippi. By that time, I'd already been to about three other schools, and I was once again the new kid on the block.

I'm grateful for the experience though. It taught me to get out there and make my own way. I had to learn how to adjust; I had to get involved, join the athletic teams, and make new friends all of my own volition, because I missed the opportunities that came automatically to the kids who had grown up together in Wilmette and had known each other since kindergarten.

And I learned to capitalize on the entrepreneurial spirit I'd first tapped into with my Little Red Wagon newspaper business at the age of four.

For several months after we moved to our new home in Wilmette, I didn't get invited to the birthday parties of any of the kids in my class at Stolp Grammar School because their mothers didn't know me. But at Christmas time, my Aunt Frieda bought me a little magic set, the kind that sold for about two bucks at the time. I learned a couple of tricks and took them to school and showed them to my new classmates.

The next thing I knew, I started getting invited to all the birthday parties. I became the main attraction, and the mothers would give me two or three bucks to do magic tricks at their children's birthday parties.

Hugh, age nine, with best friend "Tiger" at their home in Wilmette, Ill.

At a very young age, I started learning that it was up to me to make things happen, and I discovered that I was up for the challenge; I was willing to do whatever it takes. In my experience, then and now, the key word is *tenacity*.

By the time I entered high school, I had my own little gardening business with a crew of about ten guys working for me. We had all the lawns of Wilmette covered.

It was never my plan to get into showbiz. Back then, acting never entered my mind. When I attended New Trier High School in Winnetka, Illinois, and the Kemper Military School in Booneville, Missouri, my extracurricular interest never involved becoming an actor. I was an athlete. I had a natural inclination for sports. While in high school, I played on the varsity football, basketball, wrestling and track teams. I lettered in all four sports.

I suppose my only brush with anything Hollywood-related started as early as those high school days, when future screen stars Rock Hudson and Charlton Heston were fellow-schoolmates at New Trier High.

I was a high school freshman when Charlton Heston was a senior. I was on the varsity football team, and I remember one afternoon, for English Appreciation, we had to go watch Chuck Heston in a play instead of attending our usual football practice. It was four o'clock in the afternoon and I remember wondering why anybody would spend his afternoon on a stage when he could be out playing football. I certainly never expected that, years later, I would become the star of several shows on Broadway with matinees on both Wednesday and Saturday!

Maybe by watching Chuck—who would go on to become a well-known and highly respected actor—I was being shown a glimpse into my own future. But if that was a sign, I sure didn't see it at the time.

Chapter One — THE EARLY YEARS

Back then I wanted to enlist in the United States Marine Corps. My dad, a retired Marine officer, had been a captain—a horse Marine in World War I—and then became the commanding officer of the 9th Battalion USMC Reserve in Chicago. Many years later, my brother Don, serving in the Korean War, was wounded at the Reservoir. Being a part of the Marines was ingrained in both my

The Krampe Family: Hugh Sr., Hugh Jr., Don, and Edith

brother and me from very early on. Between my dad, my brother, and myself we were kind of a Marine Corps family.

When I was still a kid, I accompanied my dad to reserve training each summer at the Great Lakes Naval Base. They called us "Pup Marines." Reserve training lasted two weeks, and all the sons of the Marines had pup tents and got to practice drills just like their fathers—but with little wooden rifles. I tried to enlist when I was sixteen, but you had to have your parents' permission. My dad wanted me to get a college degree, so he wouldn't sign the papers, so that was that. But when I turned seventeen, he couldn't stop me, so I enlisted in the Corps. By that time I knew the drill as well as my dad or any of the other Marines.

About forty-five of us new Marine recruits gathered in Chicago to take the train to San Diego for Boot Camp. Our recruiting officer knew my name and face because he had reported to my father, so as we were boarding the train, he handed me an envelope filled with everyone's papers, including "meal ticks."

"Krampe," he said. "You are in charge. Have fun."

I'm sure he wasn't giving me any special consideration, and he didn't expect me to do a better job than anyone else could have. It was just convenient to hand me the envelope because I was the only recruit whose name he knew.

But I was determined to make something of the opportunity. I handed out the meal tickets, as I had been ordered, but I did more than that. I did a little drill instructing, too.

When we got to San Diego, I had everyone come off the train in formation—all four squads. The sergeant couldn't believe what he was looking at. He turned to one of the older guys, a man in his late twenties, and asked, "Who did this?"

"That kid over there," the recruit said.

I stepped up and delivered the envelope with everyone's papers. The sergeant looked it over and saw that I had everything in order. He had been expecting to waste an hour at the station getting everyone organized. But instead he just gave me a nod and said, "All right, Krampe. March them out to the bus."

That's how I became the youngest Drill Instructor in the history of the Marine Corps—a record I still hold today.

I had a lot of fun in the Marines. Boot Camp at the San Diego, CA Marine Base was intense—you don't see anything outside of the dirt and dust, the equipment and your buddies. But every Friday night, the Marines held boxing or wrestling matches at what we called "The Friday Night Smoker." We called them "Smokers" because they were held outdoors, and we received free packs of cigarettes from two or three people who represented different cigarette manufacturers.

The fights were held in the amphitheater on the USMC base, and the boxing ring was on the stage area. There were about fourteen platoons, so there were seven different fights going on.

Chapter One — **THE EARLY YEARS**

Hugh Krampe, Drill Instructor

At the Smoker, two guys from each platoon were selected to fight each other, and the random opponent was very much like what you would find in combat. That is to say, the opponent selection had absolutely nothing to do with weight, size or how you looked. We threw scraps of paper—sixty-four, if I recall—into a pith helmet. Of the sixty-four scraps of paper, there were sixty-two blanks and only two were marked with "boxer." The men who pulled out the marked scraps were the evening's boxers.

I think it was about the third or fourth week of Boot Camp when I drew the marked scrap that represented my platoon. Ours was the fifth fight. There were three three-minute rounds with a minute-and-a-half rest between rounds. Just like professional boxing.

My name was announced, so I entered the ring. I was on the thin side—about 6'1" tall and weighing in at a measly 155 pounds soaking wet. I had no idea who I would be up against, and the anticipation was a killer. Then they announced the name of the guy from the other platoon who drew the other marked scrap. I didn't know what was coming.

He got in the ring, and he was probably the biggest man I had ever seen at that point. He was a 6'8", 285-pound, huge African-American guy who had enlisted in the Marine Corps after playing the star tackle on the Texas Aggies football team. The only saving grace was that he was overweight. It was definitely not going to be a fair fight, but just as in actual combat, we had no choice of what "the enemy" looked like or how big they were.

On that particular night, John Wayne happened to visit our Friday Night Smoker because he was in town shooting a film. Here I was, this skinny runt, with this huge mountain of a man standing there as the evening's announcer introduced us. After the introductions, the announcer said, "We've got a special treat for you guys tonight. There's a guy down here making a movie and he loves the Marine Corps. He's going to referee this fight. And his name is John Wayne."

The year was 1943, and John Wayne was not yet the John Wayne Americans would grow to admire twenty years later, but he was really emerging and famous enough for us to recognize his name. It was definitely a treat. Everybody knew who he was.

In my wildest imagination, I wouldn't have thought we would meet again as fellow-actors. Who could've imagined that I would be the last person John Wayne would "shoot" on camera in the film *The Shootist* before he died. But that would be many years in the future. On *this* particular night, John Wayne entered the ring and looked at me. Then he looked up at my large opponent. That was the only time I ever saw John Wayne, "the Duke," look *up* at anybody!

Then he said, "Do you guys want to fight with my rules or the Queensbury rules?" [the official rules of boxing]

Neither of us wanted to dispute John Wayne, so we said, "Your rules, Sir!"

Chapter One — THE EARLY YEARS

"Good," he said. He gave me a little wink and instead of staying inside the ring to referee the fight, he climbed out of the ring and walked over to where the timekeeper was. He picked up the gong and rang the bell to start the fight—and that was it for almost fifteen minutes, no rounds, no time-outs. The "Duke" later told me he figured the only way this skinny little runt of a kid would have a chance against the huge guy was to outrun him!

I had a little boxing experience in the Golden Gloves, so during the fight I stuck my left fist out and had the guy chasing me around the ring until he finally fell down—not because I hit him, but because of sheer exhaustion. The crowd went crazy. I fell on top of him, and received a little copper bracelet for winning that fight. As it turns out, I'm the guy who taught Muhammad Ali "the backward shuffle!"

I had my own chance to referee Muhammad Ali himself in the Philippines, when he fought in the famous Thrilla in Manila. I showed up in my Wyatt Earp outfit, climbed into the ring, took my gun belt off, and hung it on the ropes. That was a wild fight to watch! Muhammad Ali later became a good friend of mine.

Years after my Marine Corps boxing match that John Wayne refereed, I ran into him again at a film première. By then, I was doing the *Wyatt Earp* TV series so he knew that I was an actor. I walked up to

Hugh with Muhammad Ali and George Foreman

him in the middle of a large group of people and said, "Mr. Wayne, you refereed my first boxing match."

"My God!" the Duke exclaimed. "You're the skinny little shit! I remember you!" Then he went on to tell the crowd, "This kid just kicked the shit out of the other guy who was about nine feet tall and five hundred pounds!" The Duke loved to tell that story.

I served a four-year hitch in the Marine Corps. I think it is a tremendous learning experience to serve in the Marine Corps. As the saying goes, once a Marine, always a Marine—and all the stuff that goes with it. Being a Marine is about the intense training and what you learn in terms of teamwork and relying on the guy (regardless of size!) next to you. It has to do with caring about each other and your platoon. That's how I've always tried to live my life: by caring about the people around me.

What I learned as a Marine has done a lot for me. The lessons I took away from those years I've applied to every area of my life—even my show business career. It's all the same idea: You really have to apply yourself and focus on getting the job done, and caring about the people around you.

Strangely enough, John Wayne wasn't the only introduction I had to Hollywood during my time in the Marines. When I was studying for the entrance exam for the Naval Academy at Bainbridge Naval Base in Port Deposit, Maryland, Bob Hope happened to come there to perform for us servicemen. I was put in charge of managing the stage and keeping the guys who were setting up the event in line. It was a tough job because the Marines were trying to stampede the stage to get as close to Bob Hope as possible.

Years later, after I wound up in the entertainment industry, I happened to meet Mr. Hope again at an event. I mentioned to him that we'd met before, back at Bainbridge Naval Base, and his eyebrows shot up.

"Dammit, I remember you!" he said. "What a tough son-of-a-bitch you were!"

After that, Mr. Hope invited me to various appearances he did.

It was also through the Marines that I first met Virginia Mayo, who was

Hugh with Bob Hope

the Marilyn Monroe of her day. While I was still stationed in California, I went one day to the Hollywood Canteen, where any serviceman could go and get a free meal. The Canteen was a lively, popular place for all servicemen. Everything was on the house. Bette Davis was one of its founders, and the place was run by volunteers from every segment of the movie business. On any given night, you could see starlets, actors, singers, dancers, and even agents and directors busing tables. There was nothing else like it—and all to honor our servicemen through the end of World War II. Hollywood was in its "glory days." I can still see the place, still hear the music, and still see the faces of those beautiful leading ladies and starlets. I went there often when I was on "liberty," not least of all because I was always sure to meet a few beautiful lady volunteers!

As I was standing in line one Saturday, a woman came up to me and asked if I would like to represent the Marine Corps on the *Blind Date* program. At the time, it was an extremely popular radio show long before TV. There were always four male contestants, all servicemen: one from the Army, the Navy, the Coast Guard and/or the Air Force, and one from the Marine Corps. They would compete for the attention of a beautiful young Hollywood starlet. The four servicemen contestants were always separated from the starlet by a curtain, so she had to get to know them based only on their answers to her questions. By the end of the show, she'd pick one of them—sight unseen—to take her on the "Blind Date."

So when this woman, a casting rep for the program, wanted to know if I'd be interested in representing the Marines on the next show, I said, "What would it involve?"

She told me they did the show every Monday night.

I said, "I'm sorry, ma'am, but there's no way I can do it. Marines just don't get liberty during the week."

"I'll call your commanding officer," she said. "We'll see if we can arrange something."

Two or three weeks later, my commanding officer called me into his office.

"We've got a request for you to appear on the *Blind Date* radio program," he said. "I'm willing to give you a seventy-two-hour pass, but you'll have to be back on base by the end of the day on Tuesday."

"Yes, sir," I said, and started for the door.

"Krampe!," the colonel called after me.

I turned back. "Yes, sir?"

"If you don't win, don't come back."

As it turned out, I did win—but not exactly by playing by the director's rules.

On the evening of the recording, the four of us servicemen were sitting there in our chairs on one side of the curtain. We had no idea who the actress on the other side was, but we knew she had to be someone special. After practically everything she said, the audience would burst into applause or laughter; they were completely delighted with her.

I would later discover that she was Virginia Mayo, a major star back then. She was in the process of filming *Wonder Man* with Danny Kaye, and she was an absolute bombshell.

Chapter One — THE EARLY YEARS

The director of the radio show had given us each a stack of three-by-five cards with all the questions that Virginia would be asking us over the course of the half hour. And below each question, they had prepared a stock answer for each of us. I guess they didn't expect us to come up with anything charming on the spot.

I went ahead and read my answers as was expected for most of the segment. But when we got to the final question, it was, "Why do you really want a date with me?"

I happened to be the last in line to answer, so I had some time to look down at my card. The line was something unbelievably corny that I just couldn't bring myself to say.

Finally, I heard this lovely, soft voice on the other side of the curtain ask, "Marine, why do you really want a date with me?"

I said, "Because, ma'am, if I don't win, I can't go back to my base."

And she said, "Marine . . . you got it!"

I had my blind date!

I'll never forget it. The producers of the show took Ms. Mayo and me to the famous Coconut Grove at the Ambassador Hotel. The Tommy Dorsey Orchestra was playing that evening.

Ms. Mayo was very kind to me, this kid from the Marines who had never been near a nightclub. When we sat down at our table, she asked me, "Have you ever had a Brandy Alexander?"

And I asked, "What is it?"

She just smiled and said, "You might like it." So, she ordered me my first Brandy Alexander.

We danced for a few numbers, and she told me I was a good dancer. At the end of the evening, she invited me to come down to the movie set of *Wonder Man* the next morning.

Goldwyn Studios was a revelation to me. When I arrived, Ms. Mayo sent a stunningly beautiful woman to pick me up and bring me to the set. It turned out that she was one of the Goldwyn Girls—sixteen of the most beautiful women I'd ever seen in my life, each one of them more beautiful than the one before. They were filming a big dance number, so all these girls were dressed in sequined costumes with big, feathered hats, and they came sashaying down a tall staircase. I was spellbound.

One of the girls in particular was very kind to me and very willing to sit with me and explain everything I was seeing. Her name was Karen X. Gaylord, and her family was from Minneapolis. My family had just moved there, and though I never lived there, I visited when I was on leave. So Karen and I hit it off—and boy was I glad we did!

It turned out that Karen lived in a boarding house for girls…ladies who had such a reputation for beauty and allure that they called the place the House of Seven Garbos. As in Greta Garbo, the legendary Swedish film actress who was one gorgeous woman. I ended up going there fairly often to visit Karen. Though I didn't know it then, the hand of fate was already on the table.

By 1947, World War II had been over for a couple of years, and my four-year "hitch" with the Marines was coming to an

Hugh Krampe at U.S. Naval Academy Prep School
(2nd row, 4th from right)

end. It was a very positive four years. I had taken the entrance exams for the Naval Academy and passed, winning a highly respected and coveted Fleet appointment to Annapolis.

It was a distinguished honor that many would have jumped at—but my desire was to study law, so I declined the appointment and left the service with an honorable discharge. I had my sights set on enrolling at Yale University to pursue a law career, but I needed money. I had about five months before the start of the fall semester, and I ended up deciding to kill the time in Hollywood. I figured I'd get a job, earn some bucks, and buy a car that I'd drive back to the East Coast in time to start college.

Of course, I never did get to Yale. I ended up staying in Hollywood—and the "House of Seven Garbos" had a lot to do with that decision.

Chapter Two

From Lawnmower to Leading Man

After hitchhiking across the country, I arrived in Hollywood and went to the House of Seven Garbos to pay a visit to Karen and my lady friends. The woman who ran the boarding house, Marie Cote, opened the door and said, "It's Hugh! What are you doing here?"

I told her I was just out of the Marines and looking for a way to be productive during the summer.

She said, "Come on in. You're just in time for lunch."

At that time of day, most of the girls were just getting up. They were all still in their nightgowns with their hair in curlers and no makeup. But they didn't mind having me as a guest; we had become friendly over the years.

One of the first things Marie said to me was, "Let me tell you what's happened. Just yesterday I had to fire both my gardener and the pool guy in one day. Why don't you take over for them? I'll give you free room and board. You can use the four-car garage and make it into your own cozy apartment."

That's how I became the only man living in the House of Seven Garbos.

And, naturally, the girls were constantly asking me to do little favors.

"Would you wash my car, Hugh?"

"Would you be a dear and help me with these bags?"

I was happy to oblige. And in return…well, let's just say they rewarded me handsomely!

The girls sure did test my athleticism. I lost twenty-five pounds in two weeks! But I also took on real jobs so I could sock some money away. I did odd jobs around town, including a stint as a soda jerk at the iconic Schwab's drugstore on Sunset Boulevard and Crescent Heights. Lana Turner came in often and loved my milkshakes. My previous gardening skills came in handy, and soon I had a bunch of other guys working for me and mowing lawns all over town.

I owe it to a Hollywood gal that I got my foot in the door as an actor. One of the girls I was dating not long after moving into the House of Seven Garbos was working in what we called "little theatre." These were essentially community theatres; amateur groups that put on plays, and in those days there were quite a few of them around Los Angeles.

She was in rehearsal often, so when I wanted to see her, I went and sat in on rehearsals. One night, I was sitting there in the director's home where the rehearsals were held when it became clear that the leading man wasn't going to show up for rehearsal that night. The director, who was a woman, turned to me and asked, "Hugh, would you mind standing in?"

I got up and she handed me the script. I stood there stiffly and asked, "What do I do now?"

"Well, first," the director said, "turn it around. You're holding the script upside down."

She was very patient with me and walked me through it step-by-step. "When this character finishes talking, you say this line. Then you wait for your next turn to speak. You learn the

Chapter Two — **From Lawnmower to Leading Man**

lines and then say them loud enough so they can hear you in the back row, and don't bump into the damn furniture!"

In the end, I guess I managed to get through it pretty well because when it turned out that the leading man needed an appendectomy and had to leave the play, she asked me to do the part. That was the extent of any acting lessons. But I was hooked on theatre from then on.

That was also when I decided to change my name. I was still Hugh Krampe at the time, but for some reason nobody could really pronounce it. When we did that first play, the Playbill came back and my name was misspelled. The "m" had been left out and it was spelled "Krape." Well, I didn't want to go through life being known as Hugh Krape…or Huge Krape…or Huge Krap!

So I decided to change my name.

I took one of my mother's family names—O'Brian—which kind of stuck, and that's how I became Hugh O'Brian. Here and there I would use the stage name "Jaffer Gray," but I finally settled on the name Hugh O'Brian for good.

That play, Somerset Maugham's *Home and Beauty*, was the first play I ever did. One of the people that came to see it was the drama critic for the *Los Angeles Times* who was doing a piece on what was happening in the little theatres around L.A. He gave both me and the gal I was dating, who played the leading lady, terrific reviews, and he invited us both to have lunch with him.

During lunch, he asked me, "Where did you get your training?"

"The Marine Corps," I said.

"Well, how about that! I didn't know they taught acting."

"They don't," I answered. "But they do show you how to move your ass."

That reviewer ended up introducing me to a professional company that was producing Eugene O'Neill's *Mourning Becomes Electra*. We opened at the Wilshire Ebell Theatre, which still exists. It's a pretty grand space, a Broadway-style theatre with over twelve hundred seats. All the same, I still needed to keep a day job to earn a living during the run of the show, as this was an amateur production; no one was being paid.

I had a bunch of little cards made up that said "Exterior Decorator"—which was a fancy term for a guy who mowed lawns. In the beginning, I went around doing the lawns myself. Three years later, by the time I got my first contract with Universal Studios, I had a dozen guys working for me, and we were doing most of the lawns in Beverly Hills, many of which were owned by movie stars.

With good friend Debbie Reynolds

That meant I had an "in" with a lot of celebrities—and that's how I started my lifelong friendship with Debbie Reynolds. We were never involved as anything more than dear friends, but in those days, we often acted as the other's "plus one" if there was an opening or an event we wanted to go to.

On one of those evenings, I drove Debbie home. Now Debbie's recollection of what transpired next is a little different from mine. I don't remember saying that I wanted to kiss her goodnight. When we got to her house, she said, "Hugh, I need your help."

I said, "Sure, what is it?"

Chapter Two — **From Lawnmower to Leading Man**   25

"I'm doing this film called *Singin' in the Rain* with Gene Kelly, and I have to kiss him. I've never done a kiss in a movie before." She paused. "Would you show me how to do it?"

"Okay," I said. "First of all, when you kiss me goodnight, you close your eyes and pucker up your lips. But that's not the way to do it on screen. You've got to let him come in to you, and you've got to keep your eyes open—so we can see that you *want* him. Then he comes in, and you kiss him very sweetly, and he kisses you very sweetly . . ." She seemed to like it okay.

Debbie shot the scene with Gene Kelly a few days later. It was a dolly shot, which meant that it was very complicated to set up. A dolly shot is where the actors walk during a scene and the camera crew is on a track and moves with them. If you can ever do a dolly shot in one take, everyone on the set will be grateful because it saves so much time.

Debbie and Mr. Kelly rehearsed, but when they got to the kiss, she said, "I'd rather not do this in rehearsal. I'd rather wait until we do the take."

The director and Mr. Kelly looked at each other as if to say, "Well, what can we do?" So, they went ahead and did the take.

Everything went perfectly—the dialogue, the sound, the camera. It was a beautiful take, right down to the last moment... but when they got to the end of the scene and he took her in his arms and kissed her, Debbie jerked away and said, "Ick!" Evidently, Gene Kelly had tried to stick his tongue down her throat.

Okay, that part we agree on. And since Debbie was such a beautiful date, maybe I did say I wanted to kiss her goodnight. I rather like her memory of our evening better than mine!

A few weeks later, Debbie invited me to come down to the set at MGM. She introduced me to Mr. Kelly, and he invited us both to lunch.

As we were sitting there talking, maybe fifteen minutes into the meal, Mr. Kelly looked at me and said, "Hugh, I know you from somewhere. I've seen you before. How do I know you?"

"Well, sir," I said, "I do your lawn."

I mowed Gene Kelly's lawn…Wallace Beery's lawn…and Rosalind Russell's. By the time I signed my first contract with Universal Studios a few years later, my "Exterior Decorator" business was blooming. It didn't occur to me at the time that I would soon be working as an actor opposite the very people whose lawns I mowed!

I eventually made the decision to leave my "Exterior Decorator" title because I needed a profession that would allow me to dress in nicer attire than a work shirt and a pair of Levi's. I was becoming serious about show business and I needed to be ready to take appointments or auditions at a moment's notice without having to go home to change clothes. So I decided to sell merchandise office to office out of a suitcase.

I took what few dollars I had and went down to the "garment district" in L.A. and bought a handful of items at the wholesale price. After I sold those items, I had about a hundred dollars' worth of capital, so I went back to the garment district and picked up a few ladies' blouses, neckties, cufflinks, etc. I walked up and down the Sunset Strip and became a door-to-door salesman. I'd approach the receptionist's counter at various businesses and when the receptionist asked, "How can we help you?" I'd reply by opening up my suitcase and saying, "How can I help *you*?"

One of my regular customers whom I quickly befriended was Barney Ruditsky, a well-known former NYPD police officer who had retired and set up his own private detective services agency on the Sunset Strip. Barney became a good friend and a useful contact, who eventually saved my life!

Let's backtrack a bit. After leaving the Marine Corps and getting started in Los Angeles, I met an old friend, Johnny Stompanato, a bodyguard for the famous gangster Mickey Cohen. Johnny and I first became friends when we were roommates at Kemper Military School in Booneville, Missouri. The room we were assigned to happened to be the same room that the famous actor Will Rogers had stayed in when he attended Kemper. Beneath one of the bunk beds, Johnny and I discovered a trap door that still contained some of the loot and booze Will Rogers had kept hidden.

Even at that young age at Kemper, Johnny was somewhat of a con man. In military school, we had forced marches and surprise drills. The commanding officers would wake us up in the middle of the night and march us off campus to perform these drills when we'd least expect it—sometimes as late as three in the morning—so that we would be prepared for such surprises on an actual battlefield. Johnny, however, never participated in a single surprise drill. He had maintained a romantic relationship with at least one of the nurses at Kemper's medical office, so they would tip him off when they knew that there would be a surprise drill. So whenever he received the tip, "sick boy" Johnny would check himself into the infirmary for the night and skip out on the drill.

I ran into Johnny a few years later when I was a Drill Instructor at the Marine Corps depot in San Diego. During lunch one day, one of my fellow-Drill Instructors (DIs) said, "Take a look at the chow line. Do you see anyone you recognize?"

I looked and spotted none other than Johnny Stompanato. He was hard to miss because of his slick, dark hair. "Yeah, I see him," I said. "He's still got all his hair?" My fellow-DI said, "Yeah, we got orders not to touch him. Who the hell is he?"

I found out that we had all been ordered not to lay a hand on Johnny Stompanato. I had known that Johnny's family was rumored to be able to convince anyone to do anything for them, whether it was because they were part of the Italian mafia in Chicago or whether it was for some other reason. That day we had a short, friendly conversation about what he was up to and what I was up to.

A few months after my hitch in the Marine Corps, when I was selling merchandise on the Sunset Strip, Johnny Stompanato came into my life again. I was having dinner at Ciro's nightclub one evening. Johnny came over to say hello. He was also out of the Marine Corps and living in Hollywood. We had lunch the next day and he treated me like an old friend. Then about two months later, the first problem I had with Johnny occurred. He approached me and said, "I really need your help."

"What's going on?" I asked.

"I need three hundred dollars and I've got to get it now! Can you help me?"

Three hundred dollars was a lot of money back then, but Johnny was a friend, so I pulled together what I could find and then gave him three hundred as a loan.

About a year later, Johnny contacted me and said, "I've got to see you. It's very important." Johnny picked me up in his car and we drove to the famous Dolores Drive-In on the Sunset Strip.

"I need a big hunk of money," Johnny said.

"What do you mean?" I asked.

"You probably don't have this kind of money, but I need four thousand bucks. And I need it right away. I'm asking you because I know you have a lot of friends, and you'll figure out how to get it."

I said, "What makes you think I'd do that?"

"You'll do it because of the reality of what will happen to you if you don't get it for me."

"What the hell are you talking about?" I asked.

Johnny paused. Then he said, "Do you know how much it costs to have a leg busted? Maybe fifty bucks. An arm would cost thirty-five bucks." Johnny proceeded to list a menu of ways to hurt me—whether to throw acid in my face or chop off my private parts—and what the going price was for each physical damage he could order someone to do to me. Then he drove me home.

The next day, I went to my detective friend Barney Ruditsky and told him about the situation and he knew exactly who

Chapter Two — **From Lawnmower to Leading Man**

Johnny Stompanato was and knew all about his connections with Mickey Cohen.

"Don't worry about it," said Barney. "I'll handle this."

The next day, Johnny Stompanato called me. He exclaimed, "Jesus, Hugh! We've known each other for so long. We're friends! We were roommates! I was just kidding about what I said to you last night. You shouldn't take me seriously."

It turned out that Barney and a couple of his "strong" friends had paid a visit to Johnny's apartment soon after my conversation with Barney. And without leaving any scars on Johnny's face, they beat the shit out of him. They said, "You better hope that this guy, Hugh O'Brian, never gets a scratch on his car, much less his body, and never has a conflict with you or with anyone. Because if that happens, you're going to be paralyzed for life." They left him so beat up that he could barely walk for a couple of weeks. Needless to say, Johnny Stompanato never tried to get money from me again.

Extorting money from others was always Johnny's most reliable source of income. He would date a string of married women and then threaten to tell their husbands about the affairs unless they gave him the big bucks.

When Johnny Stompanato began his affair with Lana Turner, I had already become friends with the beautiful actress. As he became increasingly possessive and menacing, she tried to get rid of him. At one point, he stormed down to Acapulco and approached Lana. She was extremely upset because he often threatened her. My protective instincts took over and I contacted a good friend of mine, Miguelito Alemán, who was the son of the President of Mexico at the time. I'm not sure what exactly transpired, but I do know that Stompanato was escorted out of the country the next day and that he never came back.

Eventually, when Lana Turner returned to her home, Stompanato started stalking her again and he was later stabbed to death when he broke into her bedroom. The question many people have asked since then is, who really murdered him? Cheryl Crane, Lana's daughter, was the one convicted of justifiable homicide and she spent only two or three years behind bars because she was a minor. Had the killer been Lana, she could have gotten a much harsher punishment, perhaps even a life sentence. Whatever the case, Johnny Stompanato was out of there!

As I sold merchandise out of my suitcase and was called into an increasing number of appointments, I realized that my theatre background gave me an advantage over actors who had only done motion pictures. In live television, the goal is to rehearse well enough so that when you go "live," you can get from point A to point B without tripping over your words or the furniture. In general, the actors who became successful in live television were the ones who had previously performed in front of live audiences. Because I got my start on the stage, I always enjoyed doing the live TV shows.

In 1951, I made my TV debut on Fireside Theatre, for which I did four episodes: "Miggles," "Going Home," "Shifting Sands," and "The Eleventh Hour." These episodes mostly flow together in my memory, but I clearly recall the longer live shows I

A Punt, a Pass and a Prayer

did, such as the ones for Playhouse 90, which required longer rehearsals as well.

Much later, in the late Sixties, another great TV experience was working on the Hallmark Hall of Fame production of "A Punt, a Pass and a Prayer." I played the quarterback. Betsy Palmer was the leading lady. I remember this set very well because we filmed the football scenes with the New York Giants, who were so thrilled—even as football players—to be featured on the show.

But I enjoyed doing several live Playhouse 90 TV shows more than other shows I worked on because it was the most dedicated to giving its actors ample time to prepare for their scenes. We had extra hours of rehearsal and the scripts were very well-written. The only problem was that on every show, there would always be an actor who had never done a live show before.

I remember during one of the live performances Zsa Zsa Gabor was supposed to come out on the stage with me to perform our shtick. But she didn't come out. The crew finally dragged her and pushed her out while she shouted, "I'm busy putting on my makeup! I haven't finished my lipstick!," which of course was seen by anyone watching the TV show across the country. But Zsa Zsa was quite a gal, and I adored her.

Originally, I had thought about the acting experience as something that might be helpful in a future legal career. But as the good reviews began to roll in, I decided to take my theatre career a little more seriously.

I enrolled at the University of California, Los Angeles, and continued to pursue more work in the theatre. I am still amazed when I think about my early days. When I started working in this business full time, which I never intended to, it was kind of a freak thing—but that's kinda been the story of my life. Fate all the way through.

But fate won't do you any good without the drive and tenacity to support it. As my stage career was getting off the ground and I was walking up and down the Sunset Strip with my suitcase full of merchandise, going office to office, I eventually walked into a building that belonged to an agency called Century Artists. I happened to sell a tie to an agent named Milo Frank, and I figured as long as we were having a conversation, I might as well invite him to the play I was doing at the time.

He agreed to come see me, and after the show he came backstage and said, "I'd like to represent you. Why don't you come to my office tomorrow? I've got a script I want you to see."

And that's how my years on the silver screen began.

Hugh with Gene Autry in Columbia Pictures'
Beyond the Purple Hills

PART II

GET ME HUGH O'BRIAN

First picture of Hugh at Universal Studios

Chapter Three

THE STUDIO DAYS

As it turned out, Milo was married to a beautiful actress named Sally Forrest, who was set to star in the next Ida Lupino picture, a film called *Never Fear*. She would be playing a bright, young, beautiful dancer who contracts polio. She becomes confined to a wheelchair, and the film is about how she deals with that tragedy in her life. Milo wanted me to read for the role of a guy in a wheelchair whom the dancer meets at the rehabilitation center and who teaches her how to manipulate her chair.

I went to Milo's office, and he gave me the script and told me which scenes he thought I should be most familiar with for the audition. I sat there for about two hours and read through the whole script, and then I asked if I could take it home with me.

Milo's assistant told me, "I'm sorry, no. We've got to give it back to Sally tonight."

"Well, then, can I borrow some paper?"

She gave me a yellow legal pad, and I sat there and copied down the whole damn script. I took it home with me, and I stayed up half the night memorizing all the scenes that my character appeared in.

I was to meet with Ida up at her home the next day. She lived only about two or three miles away and I was going up there at one o'clock to read the script with her. At the time, I was a member of the Presbyterian church in Hollywood and I stopped in before going to her place. I remember sitting there in the pew when the collection plate came around. I had maybe a buck and a half in my pocket and I hadn't eaten anything that day—and let me tell you, I was hungry—but I decided to put the buck and a half in the plate anyway. Why not? It was going toward a greater good.

After the service I went to Ida's house and by the time I knocked on her front door I could feel my stomach growling. She finally answered, and what do you think she said?

"Oh, you're just in time for lunch!"

I took that as a good omen!

Ida was very warm and pleasant. She sat me on a couch, gave me the script, and said, "Here's the scene I'd like you to look at. I'll come back in about twenty minutes, and I'd like you to read it with me."

Now, at that point, most people would have said, "I already know it by heart; I don't need to read it." But if there's one thing I learned from my dad, it's that you keep your mouth shut in certain situations.

So, I simply said, "Thank you, ma'am."

The scene Ms. Lupino had chosen for me to read was the obvious one; it was the biggest scene the character had in the film. I knew it backwards and forwards. But I just sat there and kept looking at it like I was reading it for the first time.

After twenty minutes had gone by, Ms. Lupino returned and asked if I was ready. I said, "Yes, ma'am."

"Now, have you ever done this before, Mr. O'Brian?" she asked.

"No, ma'am."

Chapter Three — **The Studio Days**

"Okay. I'm going to read Sally's part. And you follow along in your script, and when I'm done with her lines, you read yours."

Again, I kept my mouth shut.

She started the dialogue, and I went ahead and did my lines—holding the script as if I were reading it.

When we finished, she looked up at me, put her script down and said, "I've been in this business for thirty-some years. That's the best cold reading I've ever heard. You've got the part."

I'm sure she was so impressed with me because she thought I was reading it for the first time. If she had known I'd had the script all night and that I'd memorized it, she would have expected what she got.

Many years later, I saw Ida Lupino at a party and I told her the story. I asked her afterwards, "Do you think I would have still gotten the role? Would you still have hired me knowing that I had memorized it?"

And she said, "Hugh, it wouldn't have made any difference. It was preordained!" We had a good laugh over it, but who knows—maybe it was divine intervention. Most things in my life, especially my show biz career, seemed to have happened by freak accident anyway.

Once I got the part, I became very physically involved in preparing for my character and got a wheelchair to practice. Of course, the producers didn't understand why because they thought it was only a wheelchair and all you have to do is roll it around or get somebody to push. But I learned how to do one-wheel stands and how to balance from one wheel to another. I must have practiced a solid fifty hours in my wheelchair. I got to the point where I could square dance in the thing. I even took it onto a basketball court with some of my friends and learned how to play ball in it. The producers saw what I had taught myself to do and they decided to use it. They even made a special scene with me playing basketball in the chair.

That came from the lessons I learned early in life, and the lesson that stood me in good stead in Hollywood: Do whatever it takes. As long as you're not hurting somebody and as long as you're within the law, do whatever it takes to make the role stand out.

That kind of physical dedication to getting into character became my trademark. Anything I did, whether it was with a horse, gun, rope, or wheelchair, I learned how to do proficiently. It was a trait that I picked up from both my father and the Marine Corps, and it has been instrumental to my success in this business—especially when it came to that first studio contract.

The film with Ida Lupino helped to push my career to the next level. It wasn't long before I got a call from the William Morris Agency to set up a meeting with Universal. I met with the studio heads and that was it—I was given a full seven-year studio contract.

It was a tremendous time to be under contract at a Universal Studios. Your day-to-day wasn't just working in front of the camera, but you were given the opportunity to learn every facet of the movie business. Of course, it's a very different business today, but back when the contract period was in full force, actors had ample opportunities to use the studio's special features.

The studio offered boxing lessons, fencing lessons, horseback-riding lessons, and yes—acting lessons, too. We could work out in the terrific gym onsite and take a variety of dance classes as well. I even spent one whole week with Bud Westmore, Hollywood's No. 1 makeup artist, learning how to put on makeup. I was very interested in the business aspect, too, and spent about six hours a week in the publicity department. I soaked it all up. In fact, I moved within walking distance of the studio so I could get there first thing in the morning and stay until about seven at night. It became my second home and I did learn how a studio was run.

Universal provided a drama coach named Sophie Rosenstein for young actors who were put under a contract but had not accumulated a lot of acting experience. Sophie helped us earn our right to be at the studio. She was a terrific lady who looked almost like Minnie Mouse with her five-foot-two, squarish figure. Gig Young, one of the most handsome actors at the time, fell in love with Sophie, and the two of them got married.

Every day there was so much to take advantage of, and I became dedicated to learning everything I could about the business. I was always impressed with people in show business, so I enjoyed going into the commissary for lunch at the studio and seeing big stars such as Gene Kelly, Marilyn Monroe, and Kathryn Grayson.

The studio system meant a lot to me and I took every role they offered. I always figured that if I could physically perform a role, there was no reason not to take it. One of the many lessons my father instilled in me was that you have to help yourself to get ahead. And that's just what I was doing.

All of the studios—MGM, 20th Century Fox, Paramount, Warner Bros., Columbia, and Universal—had actors under contract and some of them were big names like Tony Curtis, Rock Hudson, Jeff Chandler, Glenn Ford, Tyrone Power, and Elizabeth Taylor. It was a very lucrative deal for the studios because they could rent us out. For instance, in those days, an actor who made two grand a week—which was a lot of money back then—would be rented out by the studio for twenty grand and the studio would keep the difference.

Even though you were under contract and therefore obligated to obey the beck and call of the studio, it was still a very busy and exciting time in the business. I was doing around five pictures a year those days, but you really had to work hard to get the good parts.

Early on, I got word of this fantastic role in a picture starring Rock Hudson and Anthony Quinn. The film was called *Seminole*. It was about the war we fought to take control of the Seminole Indian tribe and the Everglades in Florida where they lived.

The character I wanted to play, Kajeck, was the son of Osceola (Tony Quinn), the chief of the Seminole Indians. When his father gets wiped out, Kajeck takes control of the tribe.

I went to the director, Budd Boetticher, and said, "I'd like to play the part of the Indian chief's son."

For the first forty minutes or so of the script, the son just stands next to his father and doesn't say anything. I suggested to Budd that a dramatic look was needed and I would play the part bald. He said, "Hugh, those skullcaps look so phony."

I said, "No, I will actually shave my head, but I don't want to be put on layoff until my hair grows back." Budd thought it was a great idea, so he went to the head honcho at the studio.

I realized right then and there that I was in a pickle. I really wanted the role, but what were they going to do with me when the film wrapped and I was left with a bald head? The goal for every contract player was to work constantly, moving from one film onto the next. But, when you're under contract you only get paid forty out of fifty-two weeks. As soon as you finished a film, you were put on layoff, meaning you didn't get paid anything until you were cast in another role.

Of course, for stars like Rock Hudson, this wasn't a problem because he was in high demand. For actors new to the game, however, this was a studio system that couldn't be beat. Luckily for me, I discovered that the bald character presented a unique opportunity and could be used in my favor. After all, how many other actors were willing to shave their heads?

"I'll shave my head," I told the studio head, "but only on the condition—and this would be part of the deal—that at the end of the film you don't put me on layoff. I'll wear a wig in the next film."

Chapter Three — **The Studio Days**

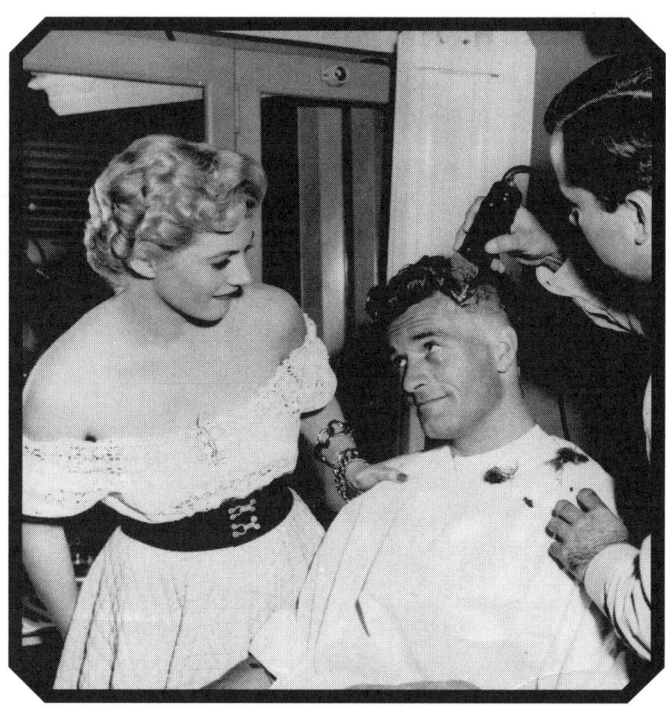

Having head shaved for Seminole. *At left, actress Anita Ekberg; right, Bud Westmore*

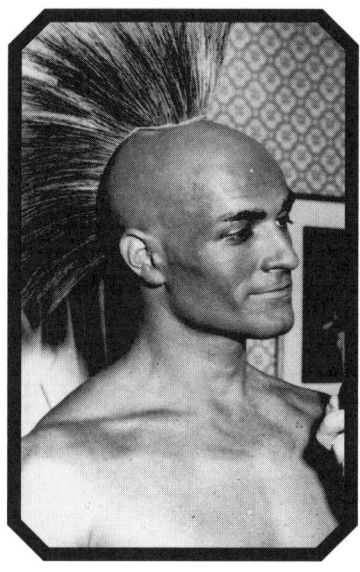

After my head was shaved

In character

And he agreed. I had it written in my contract that at the end of the film "we will *not* put you on layoff." I was the only actor to ever beat the studio system. As soon as *Seminole* finished filming, here I was with a bald head, but with five or six films now in the pipeline. What do you think they had me do? "Straight to the wig department with you, son," they told me.

Gary Cooper was always one of my idols, not just because of his acting celebrity but also because I admired his image. He was a class guy. So I had them make up a Gary Cooper wig,

Buddy Hackett, Spike Jones, and Hugh

complete with the forelock and everything, and wore it for the first film after the Rock Hudson picture. Not many people know this, but that's how I wound up doing six pictures back to back with a bald head. I wore wigs!

Although Rock Hudson and I were in the same class at New Trier High School back in Winnetka, Illinois, Rock wasn't on the football team and we ran with different crowds. I never really had a chance to get to know him back then. I certainly never imagined that I would one day be in a movie with him. And what a treat. It was wonderful working with Rock on *Seminole*. He was an extremely kind human being. Rock was a true professional on set, always on time, and he always knew his lines.

Buddy Hackett was also under contract at Universal and we wound up doing a film together called *Fireman, Save My Child*. The studio did two Abbott and Costello films each year, like clockwork, and they would know within twenty to thirty thousand dollars how much that film would bring in. This film was a comedy about firemen in San Francisco changing over from horse-drawn fire trucks to mechanized fire trucks. All of the firemen in the film were played by members of the Spike Jones Orchestra.

Just as they began filming, however, Costello grew ill. He wasn't able to come on set for the first few days. Days turned into weeks. Lou was still very sick. The producers knew that they needed to do something because the theaters and audiences were expecting another Abbott and Costello film. The studio always did two a year. So the studio heads made a decision. They said, "Let's use the fattest kid and the thinnest kid who are under contract here at Universal." And that's how Buddy Hackett ended up playing Costello, the fat one, and I was picked to play Abbott, the thin one.

It was a lot of fun filming with Buddy. We had great chemistry on screen. The producers even let him do one of his own comedy routines during the scene that takes place during the

Hugh and Buddy Hackett in the comedy
Fireman, Save My Child, *1954*

firemen's barbecue. At the end of the filming and post production, they rushed it right out into theaters. Two months later, the CEO of Universal Studios called us both into his office and told us, "We think you two make a great team and we're going to do a series of these films starring O'Brian and Hackett."

This was just after Dean Martin and Jerry Lewis broke up, and comedic actors who could make that kind of commitment were in high demand. But Buddy didn't want to do the show because he wanted to concentrate on comedy, and frankly, I wanted to do more theatre. Buddy and I just looked at each other and decided in that instant that we did not want to form a comedy team. We ended up becoming really good friends instead. We spoke regularly throughout the years and he always kept me laughing.

The last time we spoke, he asked me, "Hugh, have you ever tried Viagra?"

"No," I said. "Have you?"

"Oh yeah, it's terrific!"

And I said, "Really? Tell me about it."

"Well for one thing, I don't pee-pee on my shoes anymore."

That was his last big joke! Even in the end, he still had a great sense of humor. To this day I have a set of Buddy's golf clubs, which his wife gave to me not too long after he passed away.

It could sometimes be quite intimidating working at Universal Studios with all of these big stars running around. I remember there was a mailroom at the studio's Publicity Department with a slot for each of the contract players. Once a week someone from the PR Department would come by and count the fan mail. Of course, people like Jeff Chandler, Rock Hudson, and Tony Curtis were getting a lot of mail—their mail slots were always filled to the brim. I was getting quite a bit of fan mail myself (though I like to call it "friend mail"), but nowhere near the amount of those three. I was still doing supporting roles.

I always made sure that the people who took the trouble to write to me received a letter of thanks in return. I would go in at six or seven in the morning and take the mail out, write down the return address, and put it back in the slot. I would do this every week and by the tenth or twelfth week, there wasn't enough room in my mailbox to keep all the mail. It began to pile up! And the people who were responsible for counting it reported back to the higher-ups and said, "My God, O'Brian's getting so much fan mail, we better give him a terrific role. Everybody wants to see him!"

That's how I helped take my career to the next step, which I learned from my dad about taking the initiative to make things happen for yourself. The head of Publicity eventually discovered my trick and had a good laugh about it. In fact, when she got word of it she bought me a case of beer and took me out to lunch. Why not? She was probably thinking, here's a guy

Lucy and Hugh

who wants to be a success and knows how to take control and promote his career.

But even as my career was on an upswing, I still had to fight for certain privileges. At one point I was shooting at the studio owned by Lucille Ball and Desi Arnaz, which was right next to Paramount Studios. Lucille was vivacious, cute and hilarious, but hard as nails when she had to be. She was a savvy businesswoman, as was her husband, Desi. They did their shows at Desilu Studios, also known as RKO, which was where we filmed all the interior scenes of *Wyatt Earp*.

Chapter Three — **The Studio Days**

For the first year at RKO, I never had a dressing room. I was given something called a flipper, which was a small canvas tent right on the set where we were filming. I could enter the little tent and shut the door behind me, but it was no place to invite a visitor. There was a small sofa inside, plus a chair and a makeup table. It also had a small closet, but it was nothing like an off-stage dressing room.

One day I was having lunch with Lucy, who asked, "Why don't you have a dressing room?"

"I don't think they want me to be off the set," I said.

Lucy replied, "I'm betting it's because they don't want to pay another hundred dollars a week to rent a star's dressing room for you." Then Lucy offered me the use of her dressing room, which she thought would shame the producers into letting me have my own.

But the plan didn't work. Their comment was that with twenty to thirty pages of dialogue per day, I didn't have time to use an off-stage dressing room so there was no point in spending money to provide me with one. Lucy's generosity, however, stuck with me. She was a very giving person and handed over her dressing room as though it was no problem at all. And that was the thing—with most of these stars like Lucy. No matter how successful they were, they were all extremely kind and gracious. That's the key to having a long and lasting career. It's all in the way you treat others. That, and the size of your dressing room!

While I was under contract at Universal, I bought myself an old 1946 Pontiac convertible. One day I was driving west down Sunset Boulevard with the top down and a beautiful starlet beside me. At the top of Sunset, just between Crescent Heights and Fairfax, there was a Bank of America on the south side of the street.

We stopped at a light, and I turned to the gal and, feeling like a big shot, said, "That's where I bank my money."

Just at that moment, a man ran out of the bank holding a bag. He had a stocking over his head. As he ran out the door, he pulled the stocking off his head and threw it away. He had just robbed the bank.

Without thinking, I jumped out of the car and started chasing him down the street. His getaway car was already on the move about twenty feet ahead of him. I caught him just before he got to his "getaway," threw him up against a parked car, yanked his arm behind his back, turned him around, and marched him back up to the bank.

By the time we got back to the corner, all the security people were rushing out of the bank to chase the robber down and there he was!

They let me hang onto him, and I took him back into the bank to a back room where they took custody of him and started searching him. By then the press people started arriving.

One of the writers for the *Los Angeles Times* recognized me. He threw his hands in the air and said, "Shit! This is just a damn publicity stunt!"

The robber looked at me with wide eyes and said, "Oh, no, it's not!"

I just happened to be in the right place at the right time—and willing to do whatever it took.

It was my third year going into my fourth under contract to Universal Studios when I realized that if I wanted to be a real success in the business, I would have to make some changes. Although being under contract with Universal had a certain safety, there were some major disadvantages to being signed to a "seven-year contract."

First of all, if I wanted to get into television, I was in big trouble. I saw that the medium had a lot of potential from the beginning, but even when Universal started doing their own first television series they wouldn't let any of their contract players go near it. Absolutely not. They didn't want their contract stars to be on television because they thought that if people could see them for free on TV, why would they want to pay to see them in the movies? This is kind of funny when you think about NBC Universal today. Because where do they make most of their money? By making television series.

Universal also had a habit of trying to get you to stay for another year, but not giving you the raise that was in your seven-year contract. Not many people know why studio contracts were for seven years. The origin goes all the way back to Bette Davis. She was under contract to Warner Brothers for life. For life! The old contracts had limitless terms of employment. So Bette Davis took her case into arbitration, and eventually to court. The Screen Actors Guild finally won and ruled, "You cannot put anyone under contract for life."

The studios argued back and forth with the Guild about times and terms. The studios wanted twelve-year contracts, but they compromised and it became a maximum seven-year contract. Today, in the State of California you cannot put anybody under contract in *any* business for more than seven years. In addition, there are increments, or increases, in pay-grade each year.

So at the end of the third year going into my fourth, Universal said, "We'd like to keep you, but we want you to stay at the same salary." Here I was, doing four to six movies each year, capable of playing many different roles and perfecting skills to broaden my range, and they wanted to keep me at the same pay-grade. But I didn't lose hope. I thought this might be an opportunity to negotiate a leading role for myself, and that would lead to a few raises.

I said, "Right now, all I'm doing is playing the bad guys and second leads. Do you ever see me doing starring roles?"

Hugh O'Brian in The Cimarron Kid, *with Audie Murphy, 1951.*

Meet Me at the Fair, *with Dan Dailey, 1952*

The Brass Legend, *1956*

Chapter Three — **The Studio Days** 51

Broken Lance, with Richard Widmark (left) and Carl Benton Reid, 1954

White Feather, with Robert Wagner, 1955

They said, "What you do is fine. Leave those starring roles to Rock Hudson and Tony Curtis. You're a very good 'bad guy.' We need you to keep doing those kinds of roles."

I went to my agency for their advice, assuming that they'd be in my corner. But I was bringing in five hundred dollars a week, which meant their ten percent was making them fifty bucks a week. That's better than nothing and they didn't have to spend any time trying to "market" me. So their advice was, "We think you should stay."

I said, "I don't think so." I decided that I was either going to make it in this business on my own or not at all. I left Universal and went out into the cold old world to see if I could get movie or TV roles on my own. I did a few films with MGM and 20th Century Fox and eventually signed with Fox. I noticed many differences between Fox and Universal. At Fox, they had my name at the gate and someone would always greet me with, "Good morning, Mr. O'Brian."

The biggest difference was that I finally had my own dressing room—which turned out to be Spencer Tracy's old one. It had its own bathroom with shower and a little kitchen with its own fridge. The studio had about five to ten of those star-caliber dressing rooms and one became available. They wanted me to be near the set for the film I was working on, so they gave it to me.

What a difference between the little rag wrap-up I was used to and this dressing room, which had its own toilet and even a small bedroom area with a double bed I could lie down on. It was about the size of a trailer, similar to a motor home without the motor. There was a nice sofa inside in addition to a fold-up table, a few comfortable lawn chairs, and ample lighting. Other actors could visit to go over their lines with me in this plush dressing room.

As I began to get more starring roles, studio life became more and more hectic. Back then, actors normally worked six-day weeks because Ronald Reagan, who was the president of the Screen Actors Guild, hadn't yet lobbied for a five-day work week. As a matter of fact, hectic was an understatement!

In retrospect, I made a good business decision to cut loose from Universal. Once I was at Fox I got three films in a row and guess who one of them was with—Spencer Tracy himself! But I knew that I was really onto something when I went to Chasen's, my favorite restaurant at the time, and they started seating me at one of the three or four tables reserved for their top clientele. Sitting at one of the coveted tables, I finally thought to myself, "Gee, I think I've made it."

It was about to get even better—better beyond my wildest dreams.

Chapter Four

The First Adult Western

In 1954, I got the opportunity of a lifetime. Word was out that the studio was casting a new TV series: *The Life and Legend of Wyatt Earp*.

I'd always had a soft spot for the great American hero. The summer before I was supposed to start at Yale, my whole family packed up and moved to California. We took the southern route from the Midwest and on the way we stopped in Tombstone, Arizona. Like many of the other families traveling through, we went to Boot Hill Cemetery, O.K. Corral, and all of the other historic sites where Earp kept the peace. If you had told me then that just a handful of years later I would be playing the legendary US Marshal Wyatt Earp on television, I would have thought that you were out of your mind. At the time I had absolutely no intention of getting into this crazy business, but boy am I glad I did.

In 1954, the studio made it known to anybody interested that this was going to be the "first adult western," which I eventually defined for interviewers as a western in which the cowboy still kisses his horse, but he worries about it. The stories were going to be about people who actually lived and the wardrobe would be authentic.

I was one of about twenty people who were up for the lead role. Stuart Lake, the man who wrote Wyatt Earp's biography back in 1929, interviewed me for the part. I think he favored me for a couple of different reasons. First, he felt that there were certain physical similarities such as bone structure and height. I also think he took to me because he had been a Marine and he felt that my background as a Marine Drill Instructor would add to the character.

Wyatt Earp was a pretty stoic, cool cat who didn't make exclamations. A straightforward, serious guy, Wyatt handled every crisis and every situation in a cool manner in which he didn't appear phased. He was also a very private person, and I took care to play the role by constantly considering what Wyatt would do and how he would handle each situation.

Wyatt was born in Monmouth, Illinois, and lived in Pella, Iowa, before moving out West with his family. Back then, people moved in wagon trains. Each family paid to be a part of the train, sort of like an early Greyhound bus system. Not many people know this, but every wagon train had what you would call a "trail boss." He was the scout who knew the territory and had been there before. He knew how to handle the Indians and deal with nature. As it turned out, Wyatt Earp's father was the wagon master for his group of ten or fifteen families. So Wyatt came from a line of strong leaders—it was in his blood.

Wyatt's family came out west with a wagon train and settled in Colton, California, right next to San Bernardino. About five weeks into their stay, Wyatt decided to go back East. Why? Maybe he forgot his toothbrush or something—I never quite figured that one out. But on his way back East, he stopped to see an old friend of the family in Ellsworth, Kansas, and that's where he encountered his first "bad guys."

Chapter Four — **The First Adult Western**

Hugh O'Brian as Wyatt Earp

This is the true story on which the pilot TV episode was based. Wyatt had a friend who was sheriff and was also quite old. The bad guys—like the Thompson brothers—came to town and after having too much to drink, used their guns, and ran everybody off the streets. They terrorized the town so that even the sheriff was afraid to come out. Wyatt was the one to finally take action. He borrowed the sheriff's gun and went out to confront this group of six men. He walked right up to Ben

Thompson, who was on his horse, and said, "You need to get out of town."

Ben Thompson looked at this kid, who was about sixteen, and said, "What makes you think that we're gonna leave town because you say so?"

Wyatt replied, "If you don't, I'm gonna take you to jail."

And he said, "Oh really? You and what army?"

"Well, it's very simple," Wyatt explained. "You can shoot me, there's no doubt about that. But I guarantee, I'm gonna shoot you first. What good is it going to be if you don't have a life anymore?"

Ben looked at his brothers and said, "You hear this kid? I believe him!" And he and the others went to jail. They ended up with each having to pay a three-dollar fine and went on their way, but it certainly planted the seed of what was to become the "Legend of Wyatt Earp."

My favorite Wyatt Earp story is one that never made it into the show. It's about a young braggart who rode into town and waltzed into the Long Branch Saloon with his fancy guns with reverse handles. Wyatt was over at the old piano banging away on the ivory keys, half of which were missing. That day, Wyatt sported cuff links, which he wore once in a while. But his makeshift cuff links were generally more like small studs he used to hold his shirtsleeves together when the buttons ripped off.

The young braggart—about nineteen or twenty years old—walked into the saloon flaunting his guns. He ordered a drink at the bar and placed both of his guns on the bar top.

"You need to put your guns away," said the bartender.

"Why?" said the kid.

"Because it's against the law to wear them in this saloon."

"Who's going to make me?" said the kid.

The bartender said, "I don't know whether anybody will try to make you because nobody will want to get in the way of your bullshit."

Chapter Four — **The First Adult Western**

And the smart ass said, "Well, I'm pretty damn good with a gun so nobody had better try."

"You really think you're good?" the bartender challenged.

"Yeah. I *know* I'm good," said the young guy. "Let me show you." He spotted the piano player, but of course he didn't know it was Wyatt Earp who was playing. And the kid took his gun and shot off one of the cuff links from Wyatt's sleeve. He turned to the bartender and said, "What'd you think of that?"

The bartender said, "Can you do it again?"

And the kid said, "Of course!" And he took his gun and shot off the other cuff link. Meanwhile, Wyatt Earp continued playing without flinching.

"Now what do you think?" said the young punk.

The bartender leaned forward and said, "I think you should take your guns right behind the bar to this back alcove here where we store the booze. As soon as you enter the door, you'll see a big tub of lard about three feet to your right. Take the top off the tub. Take your guns and mix them around in the lard."

"Why in the hell would I want to do that?" said the kid.

"Well, son," said the bartender, "because when Wyatt Earp over there finishes playing the song that he's playing, he's going to take your guns and shove them up your ass!"

One of the most interesting things about Wyatt Earp's character was his marriage to Josie. Josie graduated from Stevens College in Missouri. Her roommate, as the story goes, lived in Arizona. Josie came from a Jewish family and her father owned a chain of grocery stores in Oakland. On her way home, she stopped in Tombstone with her roommate and met Sheriff Behan and they fell in love—until she met Wyatt Earp, that is. Then Wyatt and Sheriff Behan had a little discussion and Wyatt ended up marrying Josie.

Josie's father in Oakland was absolutely furious because his little Jewish princess never made it back for her graduation party. Wyatt Earp shortstopped Josie and her family was outraged.

They remained angry until the very end of his life, when Josie buried his ashes in her family's Jewish cemetery in Northern California, just west of the San Francisco airport.

A few years ago, when my wife, Virginia, and I took a trip to the Hills of Eternity Memorial Park cemetery in Colma, California, where Wyatt and Josie are buried, we contacted the cemetery to let them know that we would be arriving. We were on vacation and took our time getting up there, but when we did arrive, we discovered that the cemetery had contacted the media, the chamber of commerce, and even the mayor! A huge crowd had been waiting a few hours for me to arrive at the cemetery. They'd even set up a podium and asked me to say a few words.

Wyatt Earp led a fascinating life that included a lot of adventures even when he took off the badge. He also mined for silver and staked mining claims in the Mojave Desert. Once, he posted a sign at a busy point in the desert. The sign said something along the lines of "This land belongs to Wyatt Earp. Get your ass out of here." And nobody ever touched it! That's the kind of reputation he had.

After researching Wyatt Earp, I knew that I wanted to do the show. I was up for four other series at the time. One of them was to shoot in Africa, which would have been a thrill. But I had a feeling that it would be short-lived, and it was. The show only lasted about eight or ten episodes. The other shows weren't nearly as enticing, so I focused solely on *Wyatt Earp*. There were quite a few big names up for that role, but one way or the other I was finally the actor who was selected.

I had an argument with my agents, who thought I should take the other show because it paid twice as much as this one, meaning they'd make twice the commission. I said, "That may be true in the beginning, but Wyatt Earp actually lived. It's a tremendous story about the man, the people he knew, and the development of the West. I think it's gonna have 'legs.'" And I was right. The Wyatt Earp TV series lasted six years and led

Chapter Four — **The First Adult Western** 61

Hugh created the Wyatt Earp look

to so many other opportunities that I can't imagine what life would be like now if I had gone in the other direction.

Just when I thought my contract was agreed to by all and I was set to play Wyatt, I damn near lost it. The producers sent me to Western costume to try out the wardrobe. Some of what they had picked out was okay, but most of it wasn't. This was to be a true-life picture of the Old West. Therefore, Wyatt and the other characters needed to be dressed in authentic clothes of that period. Back in those days, there weren't any uniforms for the marshal or the sheriff. They wore what the town's businessmen wore. When Wyatt went out on horseback he wore a work shirt and the equivalent of what were Levi's in those days. You would never catch him or any other character in a fancy shirt with polka dots and frill. That look was strictly a Hollywood creation.

The biggest problem was the hat they wanted me to wear, a beige-colored number. I said, "First of all, the guys of the Old West didn't wear light-colored hats—they get dirty too damn fast. Secondly, the reason you wore a hat was to protect you from the sun. The hat should have a broad brim."

So I rejected the costume I received from wardrobe and chose an entirely different look. I picked out a simple vest and frock coat and chose a black, Spanish-style hat with a flat, wide brim. The producers flat-out rejected the entire get-up. But I stood my ground and told them that it was authentic and what I wanted to wear. I thought it would be distinctive. I was right. They finally relented and the style became an instant trademark for all adult westerns.

Frank McDonald, who was the first director for the series, was a wonderful gentleman who had his own wardrobe quirks. No matter what the weather was, he wore a large, heavy overcoat with a sweater underneath it, in addition to a muffler. Even when it was scalding hot outside, he insisted on wearing it because "it gives me insulation against the heat." Evidently, his method worked, although most of us wouldn't think so.

When Frank McDonald and the producers saw that I tried to insert authenticity into the character, they gave me a lot of artistic license with the character, including the dialogue. If there was something that didn't quite sound right, then they would let me change it to what felt like actual conversation and had

Chapter Four — **The First Adult Western**

*Hugh O'Brian as Wyatt Earp
with his great four-legged friend "Candy"*

more reality to it. I very much enjoyed having a certain element of control and ownership over the role.

The shooting schedule was exhausting, to say the least. We filmed two shows a week: one show on Monday, Tuesday, and Wednesday, and then the other on Thursday, Friday, and Saturday. If we were filming on location, I would get picked up at six o'clock in the morning, which meant that I had to set my alarm clock for five a.m. I wouldn't get home until seven or eight at night, and that's if I was lucky. Then I needed to memorize twenty pages or more for the following day and hope that I'd get at least five hours of sleep in between. In the Fifties, we worked a six-day week.

Ronald Reagan, president of the Screen Actors Guild at the time, spearheaded the Screen Actors Guild strike against a six-day week, and we finally won the right to work only a five-day week. We thought the triumph would force the producers to finally ease up a bit, but it really just meant the opposite. Instead, our producers shoved two episodes into five days. So we filmed one show on Monday and Tuesday and the other show on Thursday and Friday. We filmed the exteriors for both shows on Wednesday.

In order to survive the next day of work, I always insisted on knowing which scene we would film first. That way I could at the very least memorize my lines for that first scene and get a bit of rest. Then on set, while the crew set up for the following scene, I would memorize the lines for that one, and so forth. I developed a routine that worked around the tough schedule and I quickly learned that doing a scene in one take was "the method to the madness." An actor who could do that was a major hero to everybody, and that's essentially what I wanted to be.

Universal's drama coach, Sophie Rosenstein, helped to ensure my performance was as authentic as possible. The biggest lesson I learned from her was that "the secret to acting is not to act." We would rehearse scenes and she would critique each one to make sure that everything we said sounded as though it was being said for the very first time. That's the most basic ability required of an actor. Every emotion needs to be natural and honest. If a person *looks* like they're acting, they're not a very good actor. And Sophie, who was extremely patient, worked us very hard—especially if she felt we had a good chance of becoming a success in show business.

Chapter Four — **The First Adult Western**

Hugh O'Brian as Wyatt Earp

Sophie's coaching reinforced what I always believed about acting as a profession. Authenticity is Everything. That's why costuming was so important to me, down to the smallest detail. One of the things I learned about the Old West was that men carried only five rounds in their six-shooters, which sounds unusual to most people today. The gun's trigger was always set on an empty cylinder so that if you were in a fight or fell down, there would be no bullet under the hammer that could accidentally discharge. The guys who knew what they were doing only carried five rounds. The idea was that if you couldn't hit your target in five shots, you should leave your gun at home.

I truly enjoyed helping to create my own stunts and doing as many as the studio would allow. They frowned upon things like letting me jump out of a second-story window because I had to work the next day. Besides, we had some great stuntmen like Lauren James and Archie Butler.

For something like a fight scene, we would have the stunt men orchestrate the routine and then I would do the stunt on camera. The important thing for me was that the stuntman got paid for doing the groundwork. I always saw to it that in any show I did, the stuntman would have a chance to do a run-through of the routine so the studio would have to pay him.

One of the first scenes in the pilot was a knockdown drag-out fight with Morgan Woodward. He played Shotgun Gibbs and our characters were supposed to clash. We had a mutual understanding that this was to be one hell of a fight, and neither of us was going to use a double for it. It turned out to be a pretty good brawl! And a lot of fun—Morgan was one of my favorite actors to work with. A very likable fellow and a great example of somebody who knew how to manage his career. When he came on the set, he was ready!

In addition to doing my own stunts, I knew that if I really wanted the series to look authentic, I had to learn how to do the quick draw. I didn't want to force the editors to cut away whenever there was a gunfight. I wanted it to be realistic. In the same way that I learned how to maneuver a wheelchair for the Ida Lupino movie, I set out to become an expert at the quick draw.

I located a man, Arvo Ojala, who was well-known for making quick draw or fast draw holsters. A quick draw holster was a metal cup wrapped in leather so there was no friction. I asked Arvo to craft a double-sided one for me. He agreed, and for a very reasonable price—seventy-five dollars—which I didn't have to spare at the time. So I took the holster to my agent and said, "See if the producers will buy it for me. I want to practice on my own time and really learn how to do the fast draw for the Wyatt Earp series."

My agent came back and said, "No. The producers said that's your investment. If you want to learn how to do the quick draw, that's up to you." So after about a thousand hours of practice, I became the fastest draw in Hollywood. You could actually see, on film, that Wyatt Earp could draw, cock, and fire in less than two seconds. It became a very big promotional tool. Everybody talked about "Wyatt Earp: the fastest gun in the West."

In order to preserve authenticity, I insisted on using full loads on the set so that my gun would fire at the proper volume while filming. All rifles and pistols in movies and television use quarter loads, which release only twenty-five percent of the volume of full loads. The crew let me shoot my authentic guns, and whenever I fired, they wore earplugs to bear the big explosions. I couldn't wear earplugs or put cotton in my ears because I was in front of the camera, and although I'm glad I used full loads, I am now paying for it because I lost a lot of my hearing during those years filming *Wyatt Earp*.

Whenever there are loaded guns on set, you have to take safety precautions. For instance, the guns were never loaded until we were ready to film a scene. And we made sure that the guys knew how to handle them. Above all, we warned everyone that when they're in a gunfight, they are not to aim near anyone's head.

Somebody made this mistake with President Reagan when he was still a Hollywood actor. Somebody in a staged gunfight fired too close to his head, and as a result it really affected his hearing. I would take other safety measures when I traveled with my guns for rodeos and circuses in later years. If I took a plane, I would check them with the pilots in the cockpit and pick them up at the end of the flight. I always kept them with me because they were too valuable to lose and too valuable to misuse!

Wyatt Earp was an overnight success and about five weeks into it we were doing tremendously in the ratings and it was one of the top shows on TV. I decided to have my agent speak to them again and ask them if they would now consider giving me the seventy-five dollars for the holster "ole Wyatt" was now using every day on set. And again, word came back: "No. You bought it and it's up to you. If you don't want to use that holster, we have plenty of other holsters you can use."

Before I responded, I considered one of the many lessons my dad taught me: Never *ever* make a snap decision unless it's absolutely crucial. If something is that important, sleep on it. Give yourself time to think it through. So I went home and slept on it. The next day, I went on the set and visited our prop master and asked him, "How much stuff do we rent here?"

"All the firearms, saddles, saddle bags, canteens, and rifles," he told me.

I asked him how much it cost and he said, "It's between one thousand and twelve hundred dollars. Sometimes it's fifteen hundred a day."

"Wow! How would you like to make ten percent of that every week?" I asked.

"How?"

"Well, there's a new company called National Gun Rental. If you rent from them, you'll get ten percent of the action."

"I've never heard of them!"

"That's because I just started it today!" I took the first money I earned from the TV series *Wyatt Earp* and went out with our prop master and bought all the guns, saddles and holsters we could find. That holster alone rented for twelve bucks a week. By the end of the filming of the series, the holster gave me two thousand dollars profit. Plus, I rented out all of the other

Chapter Four — **The First Adult Western**

equipment. I guess that's why they say, "If you can't beat 'em, join 'em!"

Wyatt and his wife, Josie, ended up in Los Angeles toward the end of his life. When he died on West 17th Street in 1929, he left behind a lot of friends, many of whom would visit me on the set of our series. One of the most memorable was a man by the name of Al Jennings, who in his heyday was known as the great train robber. He was in his eighties when I met him and had been an inmate at the prison in Leavenworth, Kansas, for the past forty years. Wyatt had put him there.

The authorities finally let him out because of his age, so he left Kansas and went out West to see his old friend, Wyatt Earp. When he came on our set, it was as if he really did believe that I was the real Wyatt Earp. On the third day of his visit, he came to me and said, "I'm getting the hell out of here. This is such bullshit!"

"Oh, really?" I said.

"Yeah," he said. "You guys have gunfights every day and fights in every show. We were lucky if we got one of those a week."

"Well, where are you going?" I asked.

"I don't have any old friends. They're all dead. My family—they're all dead, too. I want to go back. The only friends I've got are in the prison so I'm going to go back to Leavenworth."

"Well, how are you going to get there?" I asked.

"Wyatt, you must think I'm stupid." And he pulled out a Greyhound bus ticket and shoved it in my face to show that he had bought a round-trip ticket. What a character! I gave him a couple hundred bucks to buy himself a few nice meals on his way back to Kansas.

The next day, I got to thinking about this old guy going back to the prison and knocking on the gate to let him back in. I picked up the phone and got the number for Leavenworth. After about two or three different people, they finally put me through to the warden. When the warden answered, he said, "Wyatt Earp? What the hell does Wyatt Earp want with me?"

"You've got a visitor who's going to show up in the next couple of days," I said. "He was a longtime tenant. His name is Al Jennings."

"Wow!, that's the best news I've heard all year," he said. "Al was the best baker we've ever had! I'm going to put him in charge of our bakery."

When Al showed up, the warden did just that. He had Al move into his home with him and his family. Every morning at the crack of dawn, the warden took Al to the prison gate of Leavenworth to start his work. And Al was in charge of that bakery until the day he died. It became known as one of the best bakeries in the USA. Stories say many guys committed crimes so they would be sent to Leavenworth just because the cakes, pies and bread were "the" best.

When we began filming the TV series, we were made very much aware of the memory of Wyatt Earp. The Old West was still present in most of our older viewers. For others, our show set the standard for how they would forever picture Wyatt Earp and that great Old West time period. Everyone involved in the show did everything they could to make it as realistic as possible. Of course, you have to have a beginning, middle, and end of a story and try to do that in a thirty-minute time period. There were some things that were fictitious. Maybe we did elaborate on some of the fight scenes for audience appeal. But whenever we could, we stuck to the truth of what did take place in the "Old West."

The show would elaborate in other ways, too. Many of the guest characters, like Ned Buntline, creator of the "Buntline Special," actually lived and his story was true, but not quite by the book. Buntline made a living by writing what they called "Penny Dreadfuls" in those days that sold for a nickel or dime. He decided that he wanted to go out West and write some

Chapter Four — **The First Adult Western**   71

stories about the guys who actually created what we now call the "Old West." Mr. Buntline got the Colt Firearms Company to make up six twelve-inch barrel pistols and took them out West. He gave one of these to Wyatt Earp. In real life, Wyatt kept the gun but ran Mr. Buntline out of town. On the TV show, we took some creative license and kept him around for quite a few episodes.

My favorite was "Gunfight at the O.K. Corral" because it was very true to the actual gunfight that took place. One of my favorite ways of getting up to speed on any historical character or event is to go back and look at the old newspapers that ran stories on events that took place. If you look at newspapers from the Old West, Arizona was a Republican state but Tombstone was Democratic. So when I read about the shootout at the O.K. Corral, I could see how different the stories were, depending on which side the newspaper was on, and tried to keep that in mind when preparing for the scene in the *Wyatt Earp* series. I use this method when looking at other events in history like World War II. Try looking at reprints of German newspapers in English at the time of Hitler to see how different publications handled obituaries—it's a very interesting way to go back in history.

The *Wyatt Earp* series ran for six years, then the producers decided that at that point they had enough *Wyatt Earp* episodes in the "can." Also, there was the major issue of whether or not to do the series in color, which cost a great deal of money. Ultimately, they didn't want to spend the extra thousand bucks but if they had, the show would be worth about three times more today.

I think *Wyatt Earp* certainly could have run a couple more years. ABC would have been happy about that. All the same, I was delighted to move on because now I was able to go out and do all of the movies, TV shows, and stage shows I hadn't been able to do because of the time constraints. I enjoyed playing the good guy, but I was ready to play the bad guy again, too.

The bad guy has a certain complexity, or broader range of emotion, that the good guy role doesn't always have. I just found it more interesting to play the villain. Not only that, but more fun, too. Nevertheless, I am proud to have played a real-life American hero and to have been a part of such a successful TV series—so successful that it was translated into German, French, Spanish, Japanese, and three other languages. It was an interesting experience to watch the dubbed version. I never knew I could speak fluent Japanese! Just imagine Wyatt dubbed into French or Chinese.

Now the story lives on, mostly with those people whose parents allowed them to stay up past eight in the evening to see the show way back when. But it also lives on in the television genre that it helped to create and popularize—the "Adult Western."

The Adult Western became the lifeblood of TV in the Fifties and Sixties, with shows like *Gunsmoke* and *Have Gun, Will Travel* becoming instant classics. By the time *Wyatt Earp* ended its seven-year run, there were a good dozen westerns on the air. I like to think we had something to do with that.

The Life and Legend of Wyatt Earp ceased production in 1961, after airing two hundred and twenty-six episodes in seven years. The show was one of the top-rated television shows in the world, and we remained close to the Top 10 for all those years. I was sad to kiss it goodbye but excited about what the future held. For years I'd wanted to try my hand at other things—like performing on Broadway again and doing more full-length films. So I hung up my saddle, put my "Buntline Special" in that seventy-five-dollar holster, and got ready to take on the world.

PART III

GET ME A HUGH O'BRIAN TYPE

Chapter Five

Broadway Lights

After Wyatt Earp wrapped, people wondered if my acting career would come to a screeching halt. It didn't. It actually turned out that playing Earp all those years on TV benefited me more than I could ever imagine. For one thing, it led to a successful stage career.

It didn't take me long to discover that there was a market for the character I'd spent six years developing. But the market wasn't only on television—it was in live shows and personal appearances all over the world. Since doing live theatre was how I'd first started in the business, appearing before a live audience always held a special place in my heart. I soon discovered I could find joy—and a large sum of money—on "the road" doing Wild West shows and making appearances all over the country as Wyatt Earp with my distinctive wardrobe and guns.

I did horse shows, rodeos, and circuses. I would perform all of my Wyatt Earp gimmicks such as the fast draw during the first half, and then sing a few songs and do magic tricks in the second half and tell a few stories. Most people had no idea I could sing, and they were skeptical that the guy who played a sharp-shootin'

Wyatt Earp on stage

cowboy could carry a tune. But I had a relatively strong voice, and my live appearances turned out to be quite popular.

The live shows paid three- to seven thousand dollars each, which added up to a hefty sum of money back then! Even as recently as a year and a half ago, I was invited to Tombstone to demonstrate the quick draw at the launch of a three-day Wyatt Earp western festival. I brought four guys with me to perform a shootout at the "O.K. Corral" in front of people. We made our verbal challenges, and then I said, "Boys, you go first." They all drew their guns and started firing. Then about five seconds into their shooting, I pulled out my trusted old ".45," fired one shot, and they all fell down. The crowd got a big kick out of that staging and even today, it never fails to amuse!

I enjoyed traveling the country with these shows because it gave me an opportunity to meet with different businesses and also speak to the Rotary, Kiwanis, Lions, Jaycees, and Optimist clubs. Eventually, my hard work—paired with my broad network of people—led to my being awarded over twenty doctorates and countless awards.

Soon, Broadway was calling. I found a real niche in musical comedy, starring in *Cactus Flower*, *Destry Rides Again*, *The Decision*, and the first Broadway revival of *Guys and Dolls*, and *The Music Man*. Suddenly I was getting offers to make appearances all over the world, and I had a ball. I also starred in the national companies of *The Music Man*, *The Odd Couple*, and *A Thousand Clowns*, to name a few.

When I was touring with *Cactus Flower,* directed by the great David Merrick, we did runs in Boston, Detroit, Chicago, San Francisco, and Los Angeles. The Chicago show sold out so quickly that the producers decided to do an open booking there instead of the normal one- or two-week run, which meant that we could play there indefinitely until the popularity of the show died down.

Years earlier, I had met Hugh Hefner when he was a young man working for *Esquire Magazine* in Chicago. Of course, Hef had become a household name! When I found out that I would be doing the show in Chicago for a three-week run, I got in touch with him, and he suggested I stay at his Chicago Playboy Mansion, which had six bedrooms besides his master suite. Hef gave me the Red room, which was next to the kitchen. That was the greatest break for me. In theatre, when the show is over and you've finished saying goodnight to everyone, there are very few restaurants that will serve food past ten o'clock at night. So having Hef's kitchen stocked with food and wine that was also open twenty-four hours a day, seven days a week, was a godsend for me.

Of course, the gals who stayed at the mansion were very beautiful, and it was nice to have one or two of them offer to help straighten my room every day. But it was the kitchen that meant the world to me. A naturally generous man and a humanitarian, Hef said, "Hugh, stay as long as you need to," which ended up being about five great months.

During my years onstage, I was fortunate enough to work under the direction of some of Broadway's biggest talents, including Abe Burrows, Michael Kidd, Alfred Lunt, and David Merrick. I was always impressed with the outstanding caliber of these directors and producers, and the opportunities that came my way by 'doing' classic shows on Broadway.

When I worked on the first revival of *Guys and Dolls* with Jean Dalrymple, the show sold out for six months. We soon received an invitation to bring the show to the White House at the request of President Lyndon B. Johnson. We shortened the show to about an hour, but kept all the girl numbers so that the Cabinet and White House staff would not be confined to see a show that ran over two hours long. We did the show in the East Room, which had a stage at the north end back then. When the show was over, the cast was invited to stay to meet the President's VIP guests.

I had brought along a pair of dice that were about four times the size of normal dice, which called for a game of craps. We all got down on our knees and had a lot of fun shooting craps in the East Room for about forty-five minutes—in the White House, of all places! Then, as people started leaving, President Johnson invited me to stay and have dinner with him and Lady Bird, who was a real hoot. .

When we got to talking, the President asked whether I would be willing to take the show to our troops in Vietnam. I said, "Absolutely. Just pull the plug." About two weeks later, I

Chapter Five — **Broadway Lights**   79

received a call from the United Service Organization (USO), which had received a message from the President that I would be willing to take our show to Vietnam.

We discussed limitations, travel, and how many people I could feasibly handle. My main concern was downsizing so that transportation within Vietnam wouldn't be such a hassle. I kept all the girl numbers in the show and selected who I believed were our twelve best "broads," who could handle the pressure of flying by chopper to three or four outposts in enemy territory seven days a week. Plus, I allowed each of them only one hand-carried bag with two to three basic wardrobe changes for the show, and I needed "broads" who could handle the situation.

A broad, by my definition, was a good no B.S. lady who knew how to take care of herself and get things done without others having to wait on her. She was smart, savvy and, the opposite of a "bitch." One of the gals who came with us was Sandy Duncan, whom I started dating seriously. We later both did shows in New York, but we separated when we had to relocate to different cities. I imagine that if we hadn't separated, we probably would have gotten married.

In Vietnam, we performed at only one Bob Hope Theatre with our largest audience of about eight hundred Marines. We averaged three shows a day and catered to audiences as small as twenty-five Marines, who generally sat on a hillside and watched us perform on a makeshift stage using eight to ten sheets of plywood.

On our way out of Vietnam, we dropped in on three aircraft carriers to do our three final shows. We used the elevator that lifts the planes up from below deck as a stage. They raised the elevator up six feet to create a stage. Across the back of the elevator deck, I strung a few sheets together to create an area where the gals could go behind to change their clothes. At our first performance on an aircraft carrier, I noticed that about twenty minutes into the show, more than half the audience had gotten up and left. I was very upset and complained to our stagehand that this had to be our worst show ever because we had lost over half of our audience. He said, "No you haven't, Hugh. Look up!" I looked up, and sure enough, the missing guys were up on the deck, looking down on the gals changing their clothes.

The girls teased the guys and shouted, "Come get it, guys!" and they lifted their boobs and bounced them around.

As a Marine, it meant a lot for me to perform for the troops. We did as many Marine Corps outposts as we could, which was very gratifying. I was very proud to do those shows. We were never under enemy fire, although we were told to leave very quickly from one Marine outpost because they were anticipating a major enemy attack. That first trip to Vietnam was quite a rewarding way to give four weeks of my career as an actor.

After President Johnson's term ended, I was invited to his LBJ ranch in Texas several times. One evening, I brought along a lady friend whom I was dating. She and I must have had a great time that night because we ended up breaking the bed. It wasn't an old bed, but it was a bed that evidently couldn't handle the energy of our new love affair!

The lady friend and I were lying there in the busted bed and after we looked at each other and saw that the other was okay, we started laughing hysterically. We had to cover our faces to control our laughter so that nobody would hear us. But of course, the bed breaking sounded almost like a detonated bomb, and we woke up the whole house.

The next morning, we arrived at breakfast fairly embarrassed. LBJ casually asked, "Anything interesting happen last night?" And nobody said a word.

As we continued our breakfast, LBJ read his newspaper quietly to himself. Then all of a sudden, his paper began to shake as though he was having a seizure-like attack! It turned out that he *was* having an attack of *laughter*. He finally put his paper down and said, "You broke the bed in there! That's one of the greatest stories I'll be able to tell!" I haven't broken any beds since then. Maybe a few heads, but no beds!

When I wasn't onstage in New York or doing appearances around the nation, I was appearing on various television shows, including *The Alfred Hitchcock Hour*, *The Dick Powell Theatre*, and *Hallmark Hall of Fame*. Being directed by Alfred Hitchcock and working with somebody of that caliber was one of my biggest thrills in this business. Hitchcock was a powerful name, but also very human. He always knew what he wanted. Hitchcock was the type of person who never minded an actor showing him how they thought a scene should be played. But the final call was always his and he did things the way he wanted them to be done. I enjoyed working with Hitchcock very much. The main lesson I learned from him was to keep my mouth shut and pay careful attention to his direction.

In 1962, I appeared on the première episode of *The Virginian*, where my character was involved in a major fight with the show's star, James Drury. Not too long into that rehearsal, everybody realized that James Drury had never done a fight scene on-screen before. Making a fight look real without

In The Virginian, *1962*

killing the other actors is an art. The bottom line is that on the set of *The Virginian*, we survived the scene without too many bruises, but it was really tough. According to the reviews that came out about our fight shortly afterward, it turned out that we delivered a pretty believable act.

In 1963, I did an episode of *Perry Mason*, which was produced by Gail Patrick Jackson, another woman whose lawn I had mowed in the residential part of Hollywood Boulevard. And in 1965, I appeared on *Bob Hope Presents the Chrysler Theatre* for a few episodes, including one with Lauren Bacall. Lauren was a great pro who was married to another pro, Humphrey Bogart. Talk about a couple who knew how to handle their careers!

I did lots of guest-starring roles in those years, but the first television series that I committed to after *Wyatt Earp* was called *Search*, in the early 1970s. My agent at William Morris had wanted to stick me into another series right away because a commission of ten percent meant a lot of money to them, but I refused because the series environment was too confining. There were too many other projects I had going so I just didn't want to commit myself to another long series. I was determined to do a few shows on Broadway, and I'm happy I did, though in hindsight I think it would have been smart to go into a series a year or two earlier than when I agreed to do *Search*.

Search only lasted for one season, but it could have been a much bigger success than it was if it weren't for the gimmicks that the writers used on the show, or the fact that three different actors rotated on the series each week. My character, along with Tony Franciosa's and Doug McClure's character, was part of a CIA group that hunted the bad guys. We wore these special medallions that conveniently captured pictures of our location on each show. The pictures would then transmit back to the CIA headquarters, which would send us a message saying, "The bad guy is behind the door" or "He's upstairs on the third floor beneath the bed."

Chapter Five — **Broadway Lights** 83

With Elke Sommer in Search *TV series, 1972*

These medallions and other electronic gimmicks made it too easy for us to nab the bad guys, who never had a chance. In fact, viewers began to cheer for the heavies because the fights were so unfair! I think if we had less "help" from the CIA headquarters the show would have been much more interesting and could have lasted a hell of a lot longer.

My life after *Wyatt Earp* was filled with interesting VIP characters I met along the way. I had the chance to meet the owner of the cosmetics company, Fabergé, which eventually led me to Cary Grant. In 1967, Cary Grant was appointed as the creative director of Fabergé for a cologne line. I happened to be in Hawaii shooting a film when I met that handsome mega star and enjoyed his witty sense of humor. I never got to know him too well, but during our limited interactions, we laughed a lot and we got along great. With Fabergé, I was highlighted in their "Man's World" promotion. Through my connections with the cosmetics company, I also developed friendships with Howard Lehman and Jim Miller, who were the major national salesmen with the company and soon became two of my best friends.

Other powerful people I've had the pleasure of knowing have included Barron and Marilyn Hilton. More than once, Barron Hilton, a friendly man, has loaded me on a plane and flown me to one of his hotels, whether it was for an opening in Madrid or an opening in Paris or even an opening in Cairo. The Marriotts were also tremendous and powerful friends, not to mention generous as well. J. Willard Marriott even took the time to visit me when I was in the hospital. I loved my jet-setter lifestyle, flying from one project to another as I was beginning to be recognized by name and given the opportunity not only to do films, but also to collaborate with creative people in other industries. Those years were certainly a productive, provocative period in my life.

Among those who became friends were The Beatles. In the mid-1960's, when The Beatles were touring the United States, I had the opportunity to visit them at a home in Brentwood. As excited as I was to meet the band, they were equally thrilled to be meeting Wyatt Earp! We had a lot of fun together during the four hours we were together. It was flattering to be in a room with them, and they acted like excited teenagers when they met me. I even performed a few magic tricks for them and they performed a few songs for us.

Not surprisingly, however, word got out that The Beatles were in the area. Suddenly, the entire house was surrounded by fans and photographers.

Chapter Five — **Broadway Lights**

The Beatles invited me to one of their Los Angeles shows. All four of them were fun-loving, light, loose guys back then. They were extremely likable and great to be around. I was in awe that they later came to my home without any big fanfare. It was a simple get-together among performers who admired each other, and it was definitely an afternoon to remember.

Hugh in Fantasy Island

Elvis Presley was another musician with whom I had a similar experience of mutual admiration. I first met him in Las Vegas at one of his shows. At the beginning of the show, Elvis recognized and introduced me as Wyatt Earp to the crowd. About three or four more times during the show, he would exclaim, "I can't believe Wyatt Earp is here! Hey Hugh, stand up again so we can all see you!"

When Elvis traveled to Los Angeles, he always stayed at the Beverly-Wilshire Hotel, which I knew well for many reasons, particularly because I'd once been a bellboy there. I met Colonel Parker, Elvis' manager, and he asked if I wanted to come on tour with Elvis and do a few one-nighters with them. I said that I'd love to try it. After about thirty one-nighters, I grew to have immense respect for artists such as Elvis who could maintain these crazy schedules during their career. Elvis would finish a show at around ten or eleven at night, then rush to his hotel to pack, leave the hotel in the middle of the night, then travel to the next city in a car or on the bus with his troupe. Then about four or five hours later, he would unload in the next city, try to catch a few hours of sleep, and then wake up about ten a.m. and do three or four press interviews before his matinee show. It was unbelievable hell. They asked me to do a few more one-nighters, but I declined because that wasn't the lifestyle I wanted, in spite of the huge money they paid you.

With James Dobson and Pamela Tiffin in Come Fly with Me, *1963*

With Shirley Eaton and Fabian in Ten Little Indians, *1965*

In the Seventies and

Chapter Five — **Broadway Lights** 87

Eighties, including *Charlie's Angels*, where I played Hugh Hefner. Hef is still one of my great friends, and because I knew him personally, the writers gave me a little liberty to make a few changes to the script. That entire experience, especially the part where I got to work with three gorgeous gals, was a lot of fun.

I also appeared in the pilot of *Fantasy Island* and then again in a few more episodes. The show's executive producer, Aaron Spelling, was an old friend and also one of the most talented people I've ever known. His show was very ambitious, and he provided a comfortable set for its actors and guests. Appearing on this show gave me a chance to return to the old streets of 20th Century Fox back when Century City was still a part of the studio. That back lot finally sold for about eleven million, which was an obscene amount of money back then, but is now only good enough to buy a small hunk of cement!

I also appeared on an episode of *The Love Boat*—another Aaron Spelling successful production—a series that I believed would be a huge success when it first began because of its unique elements. *The Love Boat* provided the audience with a great cast of characters that was its sustaining force, but also regularly brought in new stars and personalities to make each episode unique. Judging by the fact that *The Love Boat* series continued for nine years, I was right!

For many years, I happily split my time between live shows, movies and television. I was fortunate to have a great business manager, Bill Hayes. Anybody Bill managed wound up independent with a lot of money in the bank. Bill insisted that money be spent wisely, and I was happy to oblige, mostly because I was too busy working to spend it! Every extra dollar went into the bank, which I trusted Bill to invest well. And he did. I was comfortable and life was good.

I had an itch that had to be scratched—an itch to do more movies. Luckily, I didn't have to wait long. Soon I began to get offers for film roles. I was happy to be working in the movies again, especially when it allowed me the opportunity to travel around the world and collect all kinds of fun stories and experiences. Spain, Germany, England, France, Cuba, Switzerland, Mexico, Hong Kong, Africa, Canada, the Soviet Union—the movies I shot took me to some of the most beautiful and fascinating places in the world.

Hugh with Ethel Merman at the première of Advise and Consent

Doing shows outside of the United States paid very well and you were given about five hundred dollars a day per diem, which went towards hotel and meal costs, so I'd wind up with two or three thousand bucks in cash to put in my pocket. And I also got the opportunity to hobnob with some of the great Hollywood stars, from Lana Turner to John Wayne to Marilyn Monroe!

Chapter Six

On the Set

In the mid-Sixties, I had the great opportunity to costar with one of the all-time great stars, Lana Turner, in the film *Love Has Many Faces* in Acapulco, Mexico. It was a lot of fun. I was cast as Hank Walker, a beach boy gigolo who was paid by married women to make love to them. One of my favorite lines in the film is when I stand in front of a mirror in my jockey shorts, pat my tummy and say, "How long? Oh Lord, how long?" At forty, I was still in great shape—and had to be, to play opposite the Number One beautiful star, Lana Turner!

Of all the actresses I've worked with over the years, Lana was one of my favorites. She didn't act like the mega star she was; she was always very pleasant and down-to-earth. Lana said she remembered me from my days working as a soda jerk at Schwab's Drugstore on the Sunset Strip. I wasn't sure whether or not I believed her, but I'd like to think she was telling the truth...especially since she said I made the best milkshakes she'd ever had!

Unfortunately, about halfway into filming *Love Has Many Faces*, Lana became very ill. She didn't come to the set one day, then the next. After several tests at the hospital in Acapulco, they decided to send her back to Los Angeles—they weren't sure she would get the right treatment there in Acapulco. So they flew Lana back to Los Angeles, California, to Cedars-Sinai hospital where they knew she'd get proper care.

We shot all the scenes we could without her, but after a week or so, there was nothing left to film without her. We were put on "layoff." The actors, producers, director, and all the rest of the cast and crew were taken off the payroll.

Lana Turner in Love Has Many Faces, 1965

They asked if I wanted to go back to Los Angeles or stay in Mexico, and I elected to stay. Paid vacations in Acapulco don't come along every day!

So for a couple of weeks, I bummed around Acapulco enjoying a great time. I often went fishing. Once I caught a giant sea bass that was three times my size. I had a bunch of fun adventures that I still cherish today.

When Lana came back on the set a couple of weeks later, we were all very happy to see her. She put on a dress to do the first scene...and it practically fell off her. She'd lost quite a bit of weight in the hospital. Lana was already petite. The difference was striking.

Chapter Six — **On the Set**

So, we were put on layoff again, this time because the head of wardrobe, the great costume designer Edith Head, had to remake all of Lana's costumes. To this day, if you watch the film and look closely at Lana in some shots, you can see that she had lost a lot of weight.

Four or five days later, Edith had refitted Lana's wardrobe beautifully like the pro she was, and we were back "on camera." In the meantime, I had enjoyed three weeks of vacation in Acapulco all expenses paid! Not too shabby!

Over a decade later, I was in Hong Kong filming *The Game of Death*. They put the crew in a Holiday Inn, which cost about seventy dollars a night, but put the producer, the director, one or two of the production people, another star, and myself at the fancier, but very expensive, Peninsula Hotel. I received five hundred dollars per day to cover food and lodging. The hotel fee ate up most of that. So on the second day, I packed my things and moved everything over to the Holiday Inn, which was only two blocks away. That was one of the best moves I ever made—I now had four hundred extra dollars to put in my pocket each day. A bed is a bed. I couldn't care less about all the ritzy amenities!

When I filmed movies overseas, I also understood the value of having a place to go where you could get a cold beer and conversation after a long day's work—not only for me, but also for the crew at the end of each day. On the set of *The Game of Death*, each evening I consistently made up a batch of martinis and took them to the bow of the Suzie Wong Ferry, which sailed back and forth between the mainland and the island of Hong Kong. I invited the crew to join me for a cocktail reception at the end of filming each day. Little gestures like that go a long way. I always honored and appreciated our crew on every film or TV show I made, because that always made the entire filming experience much more pleasant for everyone.

Working with Bruce Lee and Chuck Norris was an exciting challenge. They were both incredible professionals, as were the other actors in *The Game of Death*. I quickly learned and applied as much karate as I could, practicing the sport for two to three hours a day. I also got along well with Kareem Abdul-Jabbar, who was a bright, wonderful gentleman. It was fun walking around the streets of Hong Kong with a guy seven feet tall! Bruce Lee, who also directed the film, was always very pleased that everyone on the set was a complete professional who could get the filming done pretty much on schedule. Not too long after we shot the first footage for *The Game of Death*, Lee passed away, and we finished the film with a "look-alike" filling in for some of his action scenes.

Working hard came hand in hand with enjoying myself. *Assassination in Rome*, which I starred in along with Cyd Charisse, was filmed in beautiful Italy. The hotels we stayed in were always on the water, so we were picked up by boat every morning to go to work. The man steering the boat would cruise right up beneath the window of our hotel and yell, "Hugh, are you ready?"

I'd go to my window and yell down, "Coming down. Coming down."

We did that for the first four days, and then on the fifth day, when the man on the boat yelled up to me and asked if I was ready, I yelled down, "Yeah, we sure are," and had my costar, Cyd Charisse, and her two gorgeous "gal pals" appear at the window with me. The crew had been wondering who I was having an affair with so we decided to give them a good laugh! Bravo, Bravo, O'Brian!

I loved doing films overseas because it gave me a chance to travel and see the world at the production companies' expense. I could really see and experience each country we filmed in. If you get a kick out of being in a completely different atmosphere, filming in other countries is fantastic. I've always enjoyed the experience of filming "all expenses paid," on location. Because I have a tremendous curiosity, it was nice to have the time to explore and figure out what makes a country tick. Some locations were more fascinating than others, but they all had their unique charm and history. I can't think of a single location in other parts of the world I didn't enjoy during my career.

When I filmed in Africa, for instance, we stayed about twelve miles north out of Nairobi, so it was exciting to have the freedom to go in and out of the city and see that awesome area. I was able to meet people and explore all areas within about a three hundred-mile radius of Nairobi. Fantastic! I also enjoyed taking some time to do charity work wherever we were, and meeting businesspeople and the people who ran the cities.

One of the movies I filmed in Kenya was called *Killer Force*, which also starred OJ Simpson, as well as Telly Savalas and Peter Fonda. OJ was an easy guy to know and also extremely popular on the set. Needless to say, the gals corralled that "ladies' man." Luckily, I could run as fast as OJ, so I got my fair share of the ladies too!

Sometimes the experiences I had while filming in foreign countries had less to do with people and more to do with the local animals. Animals have always fascinated me. I've had four-legged friends from the time I was three years old. My father, who became the adjutant of Chicago's Black Horse Troop

On set of Africa–Texas Style!*, 1967, with an Eland I had just roped*

of World War I veterans, taught me to ride horses at their armory in the city. I learned early that animals can be man's best friends. Later, as an actor, I often found myself enjoying interacting with them on various film sets.

Africa–Texas Style! was a film about two American cowboys who are hired to capture animals for a rancher's Game Ranching business. This consisted of roping all the animals you could and putting them into a corral and domesticating them to breed for food or to "showcase."

Interacting with animal costars

The film required that the animals be kept alive in a corral on the set, so I had to learn to rope the animals without hurting them.

One night, some guys came onto the set, busted down the fence, and tore open the corral so that all the animals escaped. It had taken weeks and weeks to capture them, and we all sat around moaning and groaning because we had lost our animals.

The next morning, as we prepared to bring the first animals back to the corral, the top star of the film, John Mills, stood at the corral and shouted excitedly, "You don't have to worry about roping them. They're coming back on their own!" And sure enough, the animals were trotting back on their own. They were

Chapter Six — **On the Set**

smart enough to come back to the place where they would be fed and not worry about predators.

When I filmed *Love Has Many Faces* with Lana Turner, I had to enter a bullring dressed as a matador, rope, and tie up a wild bull. When people ask me how I learned to do it, I say, "By trying it." I learned that in order to fight a wild bull, first I had to learn which

Uh, this wasn't in the script!

way he would hook his head when he charged. Whether he hooked to the left or to the right I would maneuver accordingly to avoid getting gored on the bull's first charge.

Learning how to rope a wild bull was exactly the practice I needed for *Africa–Texas Style!* where, two years later, I had to rope a Rhino, on foot.

On that film set, I was riding under a tree on horseback when a Boa Constrictor fell out of a tree and landed on top of me. My horse kicked me off and ran away, never to be seen again. The Boa Constrictor was part of the script. My carrying the huge snake around as a playmate was not. When my horse knocked me off, I found myself facing a rhinoceros charging my way. I had nothing

One scary moment!

All's Well That Ends Well

Chapter Six — **On the Set**

With costar Mickey Rooney in Ambush Bay, *1966*

except my rope, and I was scared s---less! I decided that the best thing to do was not run, but to handle the situation by using my rope. I figured out which way the rhino hooked, and tried to get the rhino to charge back toward the forest. I finally got the rope over the rhino's head as he charged me and headed for the first tree. Wrapped around the tree, he finally was tied to us.

As they say, if you can't beat 'em, join 'em

I never expected to rope a rhino to a tree, but I was certainly willing to try. Many of the action films hired me because I was willing to try anything. If a film required a lot of violence, the producers knew to call Hugh O'Brian! I mostly worked in action films because I could handle the action, plus I enjoyed performing my own stunts. Of course, I made sure the stuntmen got the pay they deserved for setting up the routines.

In one of the action scenes in *Ambush Bay*, I wound up in an irrigation ditch to avoid getting "shot" in the scene, and I found myself facing a water buffalo. I had to deal with him somehow, so I rode the water buffalo to safety! The writers oftentimes put even crazier scenes in the script, and executives and producers were eventually used to me taking risks with these wild animals. Everyone knew I was the nutty actor who was always

Who's Boss?

Hugh with the Harpy eagle in Harpy

willing to "try." Becoming known for that helped me make a few extra bucks.

I had several other dangerous animal encounters, sometimes for charity purposes. Once at a zoo, somebody made a bet that I wouldn't wrestle with a tiger. When the tiger was on my lap, I wasn't scared of him, but he was scared of me. I don't think the tiger had ever met anybody that took him on, and I was pretty well convinced that he should

Chapter Six — On the Set

do what I told him to do. So I punched him in the face so that he would know who I was and to stop snarling.

On the set of CBS's first two-hour television film, *Harpy*, the script called for a Harpy eagle to land on my arm. The Harpy eagle is the second largest bird in the world at about fifty-five pounds and a wingspan of seven feet, second only to the Condor in size. The film required an actor who had the guts to "falcon" this bird, but also required a horse that would tolerate it. My first horse lost it on the second day of my learning how to handle this. When the eagle came toward us, the horse panicked, bumped me off, and ran off and broke his leg.

An adventurous pair!

Even when I wasn't filming, I always sought adventures with animals. I once took one of my smaller dogs, "Queenie," parachuting with me. But she seemed to enjoy it. After all, if she didn't like it, she wouldn't have jumped off the plane with me!

My favorite memories were the funny mishaps that would happen on the film set every now and then. And they weren't restricted to Boa Constrictors and Rhinos! On the set of Raoul Walsh's *Saskatchewan*, I played the bad guy opposite Alan Ladd, who played a key officer of the Royal Mounted Police. We were up on location in Banff, Canada, which was fun because the studio would take care of the room and board while we stayed on location for a few weeks. Alan Ladd was not much taller than Mickey Rooney, and one of the first scenes he and I had to film together was a dolly shot (a track shot) of the two of us walking along. I was on the inside next to the track and Alan Ladd was to my right.

After we rehearsed the scene, the crew dug a trench for me to walk in so that Alan Ladd would appear to be as tall as I was. Then we went for the "take." The "take" was perfect and we managed to record the dialogue perfectly. At the end of the scene, I turned to Alan Ladd and said my final lines in the spirit of "Screw you. You'll get yours!" But when I turned to leave, I fell flat on my ass because they forgot to dig a way out of the trench!

In that same film, Shelley Winters played my lover, which took her a bit of getting used to because we had met previously under wildly different circumstances. When I was still taking odd jobs to make an extra buck here and there, I worked part time as a mailman and I happened to deliver mail to Shelley Winters' apartment building on my route, which is how I first met her. So talking to her was a little difficult at first because she was a little upset that her mailman was now playing a role opposite her in a film. Shelley Winters was difficult to get along with in the first place because she was dating Joe DiMaggio, who would often show up on set. DiMaggio was a nice guy who didn't mean to intrude, but whenever he showed up, Shelley wanted nothing more than to be with him one hundred percent of the time and didn't care about the film. It was tough to get her to rehearse, much less to film actual scenes. But eventually, she and I got along fine.

In *Saskatchewan*, just before the gunfight in which Alan Ladd kills me, I use Shelley Winters as a shield. In the scene, I was supposed to push her aside before going into the fight with Alan Ladd. But after we rehearsed the scene a few times our director, Raoul Walsh, came over and said, "I want you to do me a favor."

Chapter Six — **On the Set**

"Yes, sir," I replied.

"At the end, when you push Shelley aside, I want you to throw her as far as you can."

I took the recommendation seriously and when we redid the scene, I didn't just push Shelley Winters aside. I flung her about twenty feet! And Walsh shouted, "Take! That's a take!"

Shelley Winters may have been the big-name actress in *Saskatchewan*, but it was another starlet I became close to during filming: Marilyn Monroe. Marilyn and I first met on the set of *There's No Business Like Show Business*, which we filmed at 20th Century Fox. That same year, while I was doing *Saskatchewan*, Marilyn was also in Banff doing a film called *River of No Return* with Rory Calhoun. As it so happened, we were staying in the same hotel.

People often ask me what it was like to work with top movie stars such as Marilyn Monroe. Marilyn was a very kind and gentle woman. She wasn't the so-called "movie star" who could be obnoxious on the set. She was terrifically beautiful, even without her makeup on, and I could definitely understand her allure, but she was also very simple and somewhat innocent. Unfortunately, most of her fans didn't see that—all they saw was the glam!

Almost every morning, Marilyn and I would grab a cup of coffee together. One morning, she looked like she had been hit by a truck. She told me that every night some male fans would knock on her door hoping to get admittance to her room. She would tell them to go away but the men wouldn't.

Here she was in Banff, Canada, all by herself, bombarded by a slew of eager guys running after her. She was very sweet to me, and I took it upon myself to make sure that no one ever bothered her again. I made it very clear that if any guy were to get within ten feet of her, they would have to answer to me. I put a sign on her door and in big print wrote, "Do not touch this door; otherwise, I will come get you."—Wyatt Earp

She never had anybody knock again!

Marilyn wasn't just a beautiful woman. Underneath all of the Hollywood glamour, she was a very soft, kind, and normal person, and I was very sorry when she died so young. She should have and could have gotten so much more out of life. I recently attended an auction with my wife, and one of Marilyn's dresses sold for around six million dollars!

Jane Russell was another gorgeous actress. I met her at the Hollywood Canteen when I was still in the Marine Corps. I considered her a good friend. When I came out west after my four-year hitch in the Corps, we became even better friends. Our relationship was never anything more than platonic, similar to my relationship with Debbie Reynolds. Jane was a pal and I'd give her a lot of advice and offer her help, whether it was in regard to her landscaping or her men-scaping! I also got to know her good friend Connie Haines. They were both great gals.

During our friendship, I had taken both Jane and Connie to a Presbyterian church on Mulholland Drive. Two months before Jane passed away in 2011, she came over to our home for dinner with her beautiful daughter-in-law, Etta. Jane looked as gorgeous as ever.

Doctor Lou Evans was also a wonderful friend of mine. He was the head of that Presbyterian church I had introduced Jane and Connie to. He eventually moved to become the pastor at the Hollywood Presbyterian Church. From there, he later held the supreme honor of being the pastor of the National Cathedral in Washington, D.C.

The Man from the Alamo was a treat to shoot with Glenn Ford. We filmed that on location at the Alamo in Texas. Glenn couldn't have been nicer, and I remember my show business experiences with him because he was always so pleasant to work with and he was a former Marine. He never gave anybody any problems and always knew his lines. He was always anxious to do a scene perfectly and in the first take if possible. In fact, I can't remember

Chapter Six — **On the Set**

a single actor or actress in the "star" category I worked with who was not a complete professional. They all aimed for perfection and paid careful attention to their craft. At the "star level," actors and actresses strove for absolute quality, and that's one of the things I loved about my costars and show business in general.

On set and off, I shared many such pleasant experiences with other people in

Hugh as Lt. Lamar in The Man from the Alamo, *1953*

show business. But sometimes, there were incidents on a set that were less than pleasant. In *The Fiend Who Walked the West*, for example, Bob Evans experienced a major discomfort. At one point in the picture, I was supposed to grab Bob by the throat, throw him up against a wall, and slap the shit out of him.

But every single time I back slapped his face, Bob turned his face against my hand instead of going in the same direction of my slap the way he was supposed to. After several takes of him turning his face the wrong way, the director pulled me aside and said, "Hugh, I don't know what else to do. We've got to get this shot and get out of here. Why don't you actually make contact and slap the shit out of him?"

"First, let's discuss this with Mr. Evans," I said. So we went over to Bob and the director told him that he had asked me to

With Stephen McNally in The Fiend Who Walked the West, *1958*

make actual contact in order to help him know which way to turn his head.

Three takes later, we were finally finished with the scene, and Evans was a shaking, vomiting wreck who couldn't work for the rest of the day. That was one of the toughest scenes I ever had to do.

Slapping Bob Evans for real was tough for me to do, but many of the films I worked on required extra bravery on my part. When Buddy Hackett and I did *Fireman, Save My Child*, we endured some pretty frightening rides on the horse-driven fire wagons because we were in San Francisco where the streets inclined at about forty-five-degree angles, which we would speed down while hanging on the outside of the fire wagons. Those wagons almost put Buddy in the hospital because he was extremely uptight. I have some hilarious memories of him

Chapter Six — **On the Set**

screaming obscenities and shouting, "What the hell is this? Just find somebody else who looks like me!"

One of the most dangerous scenes I ever did was in *The Shootist*, which turned out to be John Wayne's last film. That entire film—including the process of securing the role—was quite an experience.

When *The Shootist* was being cast, many people felt that the film would be John Wayne's last because his health was deteriorating. So I contacted the producers, M. J. Frankovich and William Self, and I told them that I wanted very much to be cast in the film.

The producers said, "We understand what you're saying, but there's nothing in the film for you. Plus, we couldn't afford you."

"I'll do it for nothing," I said. "I don't care if I don't even have any lines. I just want to be in the Duke's last film."

Hugh as Pulford in The Shootist, *1976*

The producers said that they would think about it, and then a few days later, they sent me an updated script because they had written in a role for me.

In *The Shootist*, John Wayne's character decides that he doesn't want to die with his boots off! He meets with his old friend, a doctor, played by Jimmy Stewart, who tells him that he has canker, which is what cancer was called back in those days. Stewart tells Wayne that he's "on his way out" and that he has only four or five weeks left to live.

John Wayne's character is staying as a guest at the home of Lauren Bacall, whose son is played by Ron Howard (now a prolific producer). Wayne, who has decided that he doesn't want to "wait out" his death, asks the boy to bring him three people. One is Dick Boone, who has a vendetta against him because Wayne killed his brother in a gunfight. The second is Bill McKinney, the town's "bad boy" who once insulted Wayne in a bar. And the third is me—a well-known retired gunfighter, who is now a faro dealer.

All three of us wait for John Wayne at the bar, which he enters deliberately while making eye contact with each one of us. Wayne walks over to the bar and turns his back to us and orders a drink. While he does this, Bill McKinney's character, the town braggart, takes out his gun and shoots Wayne in the shoulder, throws his gun down, and starts to run out. John Wayne shoots the kid on his way out and kills him.

Then Richard Boone's character picks up the table he's sitting at, holds it in front of him as a shield and fires at Wayne. John Wayne shoots and the bullets go through the table and kill Boone.

Now John Wayne is behind the bar, and I'm the only opponent left. My character is a great marksman, but I'm exposed sitting at the faro table with my deck of cards. So I run over to the bar so that I can surprise Wayne and have a proper shootout. But as I start moving down the bar, the Wayne character sees my

Chapter Six — **On the Set**

reflection in a shot glass sitting on the bar top. He anticipates that I will approach from the corner, and what follows is one of the toughest stunts I've ever had to do in my life.

The script required me to come around the edge of the bar, and as I came into view, a bullet would smack me right in the middle of my forehead. Somebody behind the camera was hired to shoot me with a blood pellet, and everybody was questioning whether or not I should do the stunt and let the man try to shoot me between my eyes with his rifle.

We rehearsed the scene several times and then I asked the shooter to show me his ability. He shot a couple of rounds and came within an eighth of an inch of his target. But I wasn't a target. I was a living human being with two good eyes. And the scene was set up so that he wouldn't even have time to focus because he needed to shoot me as soon as I appeared around the end of the bar and came into sight.

I rehearsed the scene a few times, but it was one thing to practice it. Actually pulling off the stunt was something entirely different. I needed to figure out what to do so that I wouldn't be nervous. I spoke with the shooter and said, "We can rehearse this fifty times, but it's up to whether or not you feel that you're able to do this without being nervous."

He said, "I really think I can do it. I'm not nervous."

"Really?" I said.

"I'm not nervous," he repeated.

"Okay," I said. "We'll try it." I knew that if we pulled it off, it would become a "classic shot." But I told the director that I would only try it once. And if we didn't get it right the first time, we'd have to figure out something different.

I also knew that if the shooter missed and hit one of my eyes, I would never be able to work again. But I was willing to risk blindness to attempt this final scene with John Wayne.

I rehearsed my entrance around the edge of the bar. I mentally marked exactly where my eyes would be, and prepared myself for every possibility of error. I knew that I would not only have to turn the corner in that exact manner within a quarter of an inch of how I rehearsed it, but I would also have to keep my eyes wide open and not blink or flinch or look as though I was anticipating the bullet.

When I was ready, I said, "Okay, guys. Let's go for it. But this is it. Only one try. Let's hope we get it right."

So the director called "action!" I came around the end of the bar. And as soon as my face came around the corner, *Pow*—I got shot with the blood pellet right in the middle of my forehead.

That scene was tougher than almost any action shot I'd ever done. Jumping off a horse or jumping a few stories out of a building were something I had control over. But in this scene, I could do everything to be exactly in the right spot, but I was still completely dependent on the marksman behind the camera. *The Shootist* could very well have been *my* last film!

I was damned if I didn't and stupid if I did. But for an opportunity to play opposite John Wayne for a scene in his final film, I was willing to do what was necessary for that perfect shot.

I was the last person John Wayne shot before his death in 1979. Was it worth the risk? Absolutely. I wouldn't change it now for anything in the world. John Wayne was a real king to me.

PART IV

GET ME A YOUNG HUGH O'BRIAN

Chapter Seven

The Legend Continues

Hollywood can be a strange, surreal place. As I got older, I got fewer and fewer contract "calls," which happens to everyone in our crazy show biz. But I enjoyed making occasional guest appearances. They reminded me what a small community Hollywood really is, and that I was still somewhat a fixture in it. You don't always have to be the big star in every film, and it was nice to know that if there was a project someone was working on that I might fit into, they would call me.

In 1988, I was cast as the father of Arnold Schwarzenegger and Danny DeVito in the movie *Twins*. I guess they wanted somebody who looked physically strong enough to be Arnold's dad. It was pretty amusing to think that my character could father children as diverse as DeVito and Schwarzenegger—you don't get more physically different than those two!

The movie was a lot of fun to make. I got to know both Danny and Arnold and they were really great guys. They were punctual, prepared and professional. The movie did quite well and was nominated for several awards. It still blows my mind to think that nearly two decades later, one of my costars on that film—Arnold Schwarzenegger—who grew up in a completely different country, would become the governor of California. This must've been what a lot of Reagan's costars felt when he became President of the United States. It just goes to show you how unpredictable life can be.

The following year I reprised the role of Wyatt Earp on *Guns of Paradise*. That was also a great deal of fun and the leading man in that film, Lee Horsley, was just wonderful to work with. The show was interesting and very realistic. For the sequence I did, they really let me have my say about certain things—for example, the wardrobe, the character, and a couple of little things that I felt were phony as far as Wyatt was concerned. Just like when I originally played Earp, they trusted me and let me make some adjustments to the script and to Wyatt's wardrobe.

Even though it was short-lived, it truly was great fun to revitalize the Wyatt Earp character. It was this great bonding affair; all of us kind of came together on that—Gene Barry (as Bat Masterson) Ray Walston, Charles Frank, Charles Napier, Jack Elam, and John Schneider, among others. The crew out at MGM was really fantastic. In general, there was truly something "special" about all of these talented Hollywood old-timers, as well as some new and young faces, working together to bring back the old western characters. It wasn't just about this one show; it was about bringing back a certain feeling—a certain era—that people really felt nostalgic for.

In 1990 I was cast in *Gunsmoke: The Last Apache*, a made-for-TV movie, and over the next few years I made appearances in several television series, including *Murder, She Wrote* and *L.A. Law*.

Then, in 1994, I was asked to get involved with *Wyatt Earp: Return to Tombstone*. A lot of people ask me about this project. It generated a great deal of interest—perhaps many today are still interested. Indeed, it was an experience. I don't think I worked harder or tried more in anything I've ever done in my

Chapter Seven — **The Legend Continues**

The authentic Wyatt Earp look

life to make everything appear as realistic as possible as I did for that film.

The concept was simple, but quite interesting. Wyatt Earp returns to the town of Tombstone, Arizona, and looks back on all of his adventures with cowboys and fellow-lawmen about twenty-five years after he became a living legend, following the shootout at the O.K. Corral. We used clips from the original TV show, but also shot new footage, which we used to weave together Wyatt's experiences and memories. We wanted to recapture the flavor of the Old West, but we also decided to divide it into twenty-six hour-long episodes—just in case the TV movie spun into a series.

The producers wanted to create a certain nostalgia through this project—a nostalgia for a certain time in history, the time when the real Wyatt Earp was alive, as well as a certain time in television history. It really did work on a number of levels. The parallels between where I was in my own life and where Wyatt Earp was were also fascinating. Wyatt Earp, in the film—as in real life—went back to Tombstone to "take care of" certain things at approximately the age I was when we filmed it.

Because the show had become so dear to so many, it became this huge, collaborative effort, involving many talented individuals—individuals who really cared about the project. As a result, it came out pretty great. I only wished that some of the old-timers, like Trevor Bardette and Doug Fowley[*], could've still been alive to take part. I'm sure they would've been quite pleased. The film was shown on CBS on a Saturday night. Not only did it get the highest rating of the night, but it also got the highest rating of that entire week!

Although I have achieved my share of accomplishments in show business, there was something special about the success of *Wyatt Earp: Return to Tombstone*. It made me realize not just how much the show had touched the lives of Americans of my generation, but also how it impacted younger generations. There is a certain timeless quality to the show and its underlying concept and it really showed in the reaction we got. Wyatt Earp was more than just this fictitious character. I mean, obviously, he was a real person! But because of our part in continuing the legend, he became a part of people's lives, their childhood, their memories. To have had the opportunity to be part of the larger culture like that was truly an honor.

---

[*] Trevor Bardette had a recurring role on *The Life and Legend of Wyatt Earp*. Doug Fowley played the key supporting role of "Doc" Holiday.

Chapter Seven — **The Legend Continues**

Revisiting the past in Wyatt Earp: Return to Tombstone

A few years ago, I got to visit Monmouth, Illinois, for the first time. On Saturday, August 8, 2008, the city celebrated the 160th birthday of its favorite son, Wyatt Earp. Over a thousand fans and dignitaries, as well as a handful of Earp's descendants, attended the event. Rod Davies, the Mayor of Monmouth, told the crowd, "It is a great honor to have Hugh O'Brian here today. He is Wyatt Earp to millions of people." We were treated to a delicious luncheon at The Cloud Nine, which I thought was fitting, as I was on cloud nine myself when Mayor Davies gave me a key to the city!

As I told the reporters that day, I have a great deal of respect for Wyatt Earp and the Wyatt Earp character. It's about helping people. That's how I've always viewed Wyatt, and I always will.

Acting has changed quite a bit from when I first put on Earp's black hat and holster all those years ago. Today, if an actor says something outrageous on his cell phone, his words can travel across the world and be considered newsworthy. Politicians and entertainers alike share personal tidbits—and in the case of more than one congressman, intimate photos—with their constituents and fans. The President of the United States even started to conduct "Twitter Town Halls," giving all Americans access to something that was once very exclusive. News outlets have become so accessible that a reporter can get his story out much faster, and to a greater audience, than he could thirty years ago. Debating whether this is good or bad is futile because it's now a fact of life.

When I started out in show business, there was a fair share of celebrity journalism and paparazzi, but not to the extent that there is today. As of this writing, Charlie Sheen lives just up the street from me, and though I rarely see him, I can usually tell when he's home because suddenly, two or three helicopters will fly overhead and a slew of cars will be parked up on Mulholland Drive. If you think about it, that's really frightening. Sheen, though he is something of a larger-than-life figure, is still just a human being. The event that attracts all of this press, and even gets helicopters to come, is still just a man getting home from work—something that millions of people do every day without fanfare.

When you think about the tragic end to Princess Diana's life, the poor girl hounded by all that paparazzi, you really have to step back and think about our culture and how insane it has become. The desire to get close to celebrities has become predatory, almost a bloodthirsty quest.

My generation of actors had more privacy in our private lives than actors do today, although I still had my share of stalkers as well. I was pretty firm in the way I handled them. About three weeks after I first bought the house that I have now, for example, I went outside to go for a swim in our pool and I found a man up in a tree taking photographs of me. That was an unpleasant surprise! I threw him and his camera into the pool. I don't think he'll ever come again—wet or dry!

The paparazzi used to consist mostly of people who worked legitimately for news organizations that featured celebrity stories. Today, however, there are hundreds of people who follow celebrities and snap photos even though they're not on the payroll of a magazine or news outlet. The industry now monetarily rewards anybody who can provide an unusual picture or video. The more pictures these amateurs take, the better their chances are of capturing something worth selling on the market, like a celebrity putting a spoonful of food in his mouth. And in order to capture the most unique photographs, these people have become increasingly intrusive.

These days you not only have to worry about large, expensive, telescopic camera lenses; you also have to be aware of cell phones, many of which can take high-quality, professional shots. That's just the nature of the business. When you think about how many thousands of dollars a single photograph of a celebrity's wedding, or newborn baby, can fetch, you understand why these photographers and gossip columnists are so cutthroat. They will follow you into a restaurant's bathroom, quite often show up at a theatre, or clamor for any other so-called "celebrity torment."

But it's not just the journalists who have changed. They are just trying to satisfy the demands of the public. Fans nowadays expect more. It is not enough for them to see the films and read interviews in magazines or watch them on TV—they want to become intimate with their favorite performers. They want to see the homes of the actors; they want to know all of their secrets. They want to feel like celebrities are their best friends and family members. There is this entire culture of escapism. A lot of people aren't satisfied just to live their own lives. And the funny thing is, all of this new technology just exposes the sometimes unexciting aspects of celebrities' lives! But this is what the fans want to see.

When the paparazzi followed me around, I found that the quickest way to deflect them was to stand still and give them five minutes to capture their footage. Then they could leave happy and I could avoid being followed around all day. Of course, there were often exceptions that undermined that strategy.

When I was in Naples, Italy, for a film, my leading lady and I went to a restaurant to have dinner, where we were confronted with about twenty or thirty photographers who had somehow been given the name of the restaurant where we had our reservation. I addressed the paparazzi and said, "Okay, guys. I'll give you five minutes. Take all the photographs you want for five minutes then that's it. Okay?"

"Good thinking, Signor O'Brian!" said the photographers, who happily snapped away. Then as I was ready to enter the restaurant, they yelled, "One more! One more!"

I relented and gave them a couple more minutes. Then I said, "Okay guys, PLEASE leave us alone, we want to enjoy a quiet dinner."

About fifteen minutes into our meal, I noticed one of the paparazzi sitting in a corner booth twenty feet up from where we were. He was leaning toward us and taking photographs during our meal. He would wait until I was putting a fork full of food in my mouth and then take a picture. I looked over at him and said, "Come here, please."

Chapter Seven — **The Legend Continues**

The photographer was a little afraid, but I continued to insist that he come to our table. The manager guided him over, and I said, "Have you got enough pictures?"

The paparazzi said, "No. We can always use more."

"Okay," I said. "Take a couple more pictures now, but then don't bother us again. Otherwise, I will get very mad at you. Got it?"

"Sí! Sí!" he said, and clicked his camera button a few more times until I said "Okay. You have enough."

The photographer left the restaurant, but twenty minutes later I spotted him in the corner trying to take more pictures. I said to the gal I was with, "Excuse me. I'll be back in a minute."

I walked over to the photographer, grabbed him by his shirt and his neck, escorted him outside to the wharf, and threw him in the water.

All the paparazzi "got the message" and left me alone after that!

The issues celebrities face today with the media are merely a by-product of our freedom of communication. It's a double-edged sword. One of the reasons our country is so great is because we champion freedom of the press; it also means that the paparazzi have precious few restrictions.

We are very fortunate to live in this great country. The United States of America is a country where you can make anything happen that you want, if you put your mind and heart to it. You've got the freedom to choose what you go after, and you have the freedom to decide how you go after it. It really is at your disposal to do whatever it takes and to achieve whatever you want. This is unique to our great country. And that's why I love America so!

But if we are fortunate, then we are also responsible for doing something with that fortune. Throughout my career, I have never lost sight of my civic and philanthropic opportunities to those who are less fortunate. This desire to be of service to others led me to create HOBY—Hugh O'Brian Youth Leadership—an organization that has prospered for more than sixty years—and given me some of my very best experiences.

It may sound crazy, but a cocktail party changed my life.

Chapter Eight

Hugh O'Brian Youth Leadership (HOBY)

It all started at a UCLA (University of California at Los Angeles) cocktail reception in 1958.

I stood in a receiving line to shake the hand of Norman Cousins, who was the editor of the *Saturday Review of Literature,* **the** "think tank" magazine of its time. I was invited to the reception by the magazine staff, who decided to host a reception for subscribers living in the L.A. area. *Saturday Review* always had excellent articles written by some of the greatest thinkers from around the world. I guess you could compare it to the *Atlantic Monthly,* but it was more of a "think tank" publication.

Norman was a Class A editor and raised the standards for literary publications. He was one of those sharp-as-a-tack, jack-of-all-trades type who, in addition to being brilliant, worked tirelessly for a number of causes, all of which promoted the ultimate cause of world peace. He was an outspoken advocate of nuclear disarmament, but above all else he was an optimist who truly believed in the power of the human spirit.

When he walked down the receiving line, shaking hands, he paused for a bit when he got to me. He was wearing a smart outfit and had a confident stance, but his eyes gave away who he really was. He had these very kind, warm eyes that sparkled and you could just tell that he was a great and caring person—that he really believed deep down in all of the grandiose things he talked about, and that he really was an idealist at heart. You could also tell that he was a really passionate individual. It's really true what they say about the eyes being the windows to one's soul.

As he shook my hand, he took a good look at me and said, "You've got to be kidding. Television's Wyatt Earp reads the *Saturday Review of Literature?*"

I said, "Yes, sir. I sure do."

"That's fantastic!" said Norman, who then invited me to have a cup of coffee with him after he finished the receiving line.

Later that evening over coffee, Norman Cousins asked whether I ever traveled to New York. I told him that I visited New York five or six times a year. He suggested that I let him know when I was going there next so that we could have breakfast or lunch together. Now, I usually try to keep my business affairs and personal affairs separate. I considered going to New York as business and having to travel across the country as often as I did, I tried to minimize any extra engagements when I was there. But, like I said, Norman was special, and I looked forward to our get-together.

During my third visit with Norman in New York, I found out that he had just returned from visiting Dr. Albert Schweitzer, a physician and humanitarian who had been awarded the Nobel Peace Prize six years earlier, in 1952. It was Norman's second visit to Schweitzer's clinic in Africa and you could tell that he had been moved by what he'd seen and experienced. I had read and admired Norman's articles about Dr. Albert Schweitzer. Schweitzer's philosophy, "reverence for life," really intrigued me. At some point during that lunch, I said, "Boy, there's a real 'King' I'd like to meet some day."

"Then just go on over and say hello," said Norman. "There are no fences. I'm sure you'd be welcome."

Chapter Eight — **Hugh O'Brian Youth Leadership (HOBY)**

"Right," I said, chuckling. "I'll just drop off in the middle of the jungle and try to find him!"

About five weeks after that lunch with Norman, I received a letter from Dr. Albert Schweitzer inviting me to visit him at his clinic in Lambaréné, Africa. At the time I was headlining a circus in Winnipeg, Canada. The message was short and to the point. It read: "Dr. O'Brian and his party would be welcome at any time."

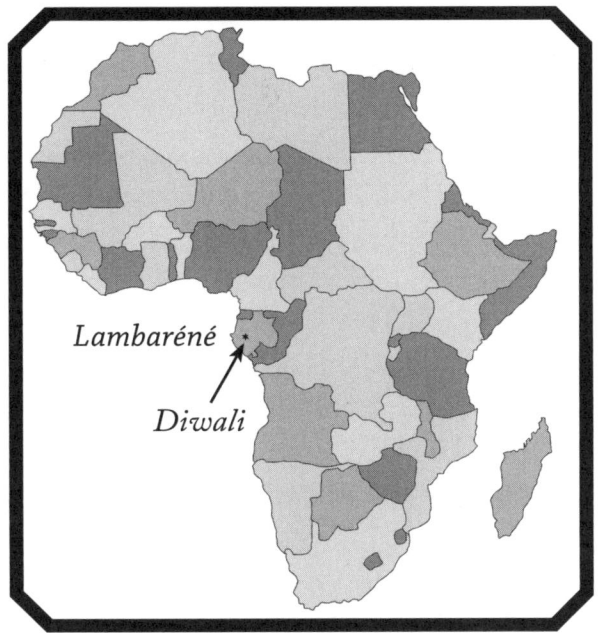

I couldn't believe it. Schweitzer was a brilliant scientist and world-renowned humanitarian, doing all of his amazing, life-changing work halfway around the world and he invited me to visit him?

In 1958, international air travel from the United States to Europe hadn't been available for very long, so it was quite a challenge to travel halfway around the globe.

It took me about ten days to get all of my affairs sorted out and clear my schedule for the trip. Before I knew it, I was on a plane landing in Diwali, which is right under the hook of Africa in Cameroon. I then boarded a "bush plane" (a very small prop plane). When the "bush" plane landed on the short dirt air strip, the plane literally touched the tip of the jungle at the end of the short runway. I was concerned that we wouldn't be able to stop in time.

I vividly remember stepping out of that plane. It was an incredible feeling, like I had literally stepped into another world.

I loved to read and I had read a great deal on many different subjects. I read travel magazines regularly, as well as history and adventure books. As an actor, you are constantly encouraged to be different people, put yourself in different mindsets, take on different struggles. You'd think that I would be ready to take anything on. That I would take each new challenge and new scenario in stride. Boy, was I wrong!

The air was very hot and dusty but what really struck me was the smell. In the modern times we live in, we really don't encounter a lot of strange odors. There is so much sanitizing that takes place nowadays—from the really powerful cleaning products that are used to perfumes and deodorants—that all "natural" smells are pretty much eliminated. When I got off the plane at Diwali, it was the smell that greeted me. It was a very rich smell, reflecting the diversity of the place. It was a thick, smoky smell, containing traces of earth and vegetation and sweat.

From Diwali, I was supposed to take a boat to Lambaréné, which is on the bank of the Ogooué River, and is about as wide as the Mississippi. The water was a greenish-brown, the green mostly a reflection of the surrounding rainforest. I remember the sound of the water lapping at our boat. There was the song of birds and chatter of critters, but no trucks or cars or other city noises. An English gentleman appeared in a pith helmet, khaki shirt, and khaki pants. This big old Boy Scout asked me to call him Dr. Catchpool.

Dr. Catchpool led me to a "pirogue"—a large canoe-like boat carved out of a huge log. I was escorted to the back of the pirogue to a seat in front of Dr. Catchpool. In front of me were six African natives who had two things in common: the color of their skin, and major bandages all over their bodies. They were wearing T-shirts and baseball caps and greeted me with such great smiles. They each held a paddle in their hands, and when

Chapter Eight — **Hugh O'Brian Youth Leadership (HOBY)**

I spotted an extra paddle I picked it up and started paddling along with them, listening to their terrific chant as we headed upstream toward the clinic. They were very kind and humored my efforts. Although I was in fine shape at the time, I found myself somewhat out of breath after the four-mile paddle upstream!

I began to take note of the cuts, markings, and bandages on several different parts of their bodies. At first I wondered if this was part of the tribal culture, some kind of rite of passage that all the men had to undergo. It turned out that these men were six lepers from the nearby leper colony, and powering the pirogue to pick up visitors was their way of repaying Dr. Schweitzer for their treatment. Not only that, but these men had prominent positions in the colony: they were the top six and becoming one of "Schweitzer's paddlers" was considered to be a great honor.

It was humbling to see all of this. I was first struck by the meager means these individuals had to live off of. In America, if you're lucky, you have health insurance to take care of you when you're sick. Moreover, with all the knowledge and technology we have today, there is also a great deal of preventative care, early diagnosis and, in general, a great deal of awareness about health matters. You almost never hear of anyone having leprosy in the US anymore.

But I was also humbled by Dr. Schweitzer himself, a man who saw all the world's suffering, and decided to devote his life to doing something about it. He was just one man but his life made a great deal of difference in the lives of millions of others!

Albert Schweitzer was a German doctor who had previously lived in Alsace-Lorraine on the border of Germany and France, where he had a very successful practice. One morning, Schweitzer woke up, turned to his wife, and said, "I have a 'calling.' Let's go to Africa, where they have a great need, and let's set up a clinic among the natives." And just like that the two of them gave up everything and relinquished their comfortable lives to relocate to this jungle.

We were now approaching Dr. Schweitzer's clinic in the pirogue. When we paddled up to the shore, I was surprised to see only a few shacks. There were no buildings that would suffice for a clinic in the United States. The natives—including many from the leper colony—came from about a thousand-mile radius hoping to receive treatment from Schweitzer, the "Great Doctor."

Dr. Albert Schweitzer

Albert Schweitzer lived in one of the shacks, which was also his office. His desk was stacked with about eight piles of paper. There was no electricity. Light at the clinic was provided by fire or kerosene lamps. It amazed me how in the middle of a jungle there was this pristine order and attention to detail. The papers turned out to be letters that people had written to him in six or seven different languages.

Schweitzer spent a minimum of three hours every night responding in longhand to every single letter he had received. I was amazed at how much time and effort it took to acknowledge the contributions of these people, and more so at how much support it took from private individuals to get something like Schweitzer's "clinic" up and running. Schweitzer was a genius

Chapter Eight — **Hugh O'Brian Youth Leadership (HOBY)**

in his own right, and it got me to thinking about what they say about genius: "one percent inspiration, ninety-nine percent perspiration."

I spent my first evening at the clinic sitting with Albert Schweitzer at his desk. He encouraged me to talk about anything and everything. As he told me about how he founded his clinic and about his visions for what he wanted to accomplish, I noticed a trail of ants walking across the desk in front of me. They marched in formation, like a line of Marines. For whatever reason, as I listened to Schweitzer talk about "his calling," I took my thumb and smashed a couple of ants.

Schweitzer stopped mid-sentence, looked at me and said, "Why did you do that? Those are my ants!" I clearly had a lot to learn from him.

While I was there, I enjoyed quite a bit of hands-on experience, and I did a lot of observing and reflecting. During the day I helped build baby cribs, pass out food, whatever. In the afternoons I went upstream to where the leper colony was and spent time, helping where I could. I enjoyed anywhere from two to three hours with Schweitzer each night in his little shack. He shared his story with me, all of the struggles he'd had in getting where he was, as well as his philosophy, "reverence for life," and his outlook on life.

Although he had a very positive, "glass-half-full" attitude toward life, he was quite alarmed by the world affairs. He had shared with me his deep concerns about "the bomb"—an issue that was also near and dear to our mutual friend Norman Cousins—how not only did the US have it (he never just said "United States," but always took care to say "United States of America"), but Russia and probably three or four other countries did too. He told me that he really felt that of all the countries, the United States of America was the only one that had the power to really do something to prevent the destruction of civilization as we knew it.

Schweitzer also had a tremendous passion for youth. He thought nothing had really been done to reach out to young people and help develop positive attitudes and build leaders for the future. I was quite amazed when he said this; I would've thought that such a renowned scientist would be speaking about something more, well, scientific. Instead, he really got me to see how important it was to invest in the future of young people, not just cutting-edge medicine or technology. Here was a great thinker who truly believed in the potential that lies in each human being, especially our young ones.

The entire learning experience was fantastic, and when it came time to leave, Dr. Schweitzer took me down to the river where the pirogue was waiting with the lepers ready to paddle me downstream away from Lambaréné. Schweitzer, in his white pith helmet, white shirt, white pants, little black bowtie, and huge walrus mustache, stood between me and the river. He took my hands in his and squeezed them earnestly for a good two or three minutes—the most awkward minutes I've ever experienced.

Without letting go of my hands, Schweitzer, with his piercing grey eyes, stared intently at me and finally said, "Hugh, what are you going to do with the time we've spent together?"

I was rather stunned by the question. It didn't occur to me that there was something I could, or should, be doing. How was I expected to follow in the footsteps of this incredible man, this brilliant doctor who had a grand vision? I was Wyatt Earp on television, sure, but this man was a real-life hero. When he asked me that question, I felt like the wind had been knocked out of me. I had absolutely no idea what I was going to do.

Dr. Schweitzer helped me into the pirogue. The paddlers took off, and about every twenty yards or so, I turned around to look back, where Albert Schweitzer still stood waving and watching me go. He remained there on the bank watching me until the pirogue went around the first bend in the river and he was finally out of my sight. He had to have spent about twenty

Chapter Eight — **Hugh O'Brian Youth Leadership (HOBY)**

minutes just standing there, watching me drift away, with such great expectations.

My plane ride back to the United States took nearly two days—this was back before the age of jets—so I had a lot of time to think about my experience. Unlike my fellow-passengers who tried to sleep off the long journey, I could barely sit still, let alone think about sleep. My mind was buzzing. My heart was practically bursting. I was deeply touched by the experience I had just had. I couldn't stop seeing the faces of the lives touched by Schweitzer, who, after all, was just one man.

I couldn't erase the image of him staring intently into my eyes. I couldn't shake off the conviction I felt when he asked me what I was going to do with my experience. I remembered, too, the words he said during several of our sessions: "The most important thing in education is teaching young people to think for themselves." I knew I wanted to begin something to motivate youth to become future leaders, so I began to make notes. When I reached Los Angeles I made a bunch of phone calls.

I wanted to create a motivational program by my own efforts and to focus on motivating young people, partly because of what Schweitzer had said, but also because the "youth" was my "audience," on TV at least. It wasn't that I had no involvement in the community. On the contrary. I was on the national board of the Boys' Club, and I was the international chairman of the Cystic Fibrosis Foundation and the California Chairman of the Board of the American Cancer Society. But in those cases I was just like a glorified volunteer, running around patting other volunteers on the back. I had never run my own project. I decided that I wanted to really create something that would make or break by my own efforts.

A few weeks after I got back, I got a group of people together and called on my attorney, my accountant, and other friends in business to help me. I decided I wanted to start a program that focused on tenth-graders, because that was such a year of growth for me when I was in high school. They all thought I was absolutely nuts! When they heard that I wanted to work with fifteen-year-olds, they looked at me like I'd gone mad and said, "Hugh, you realize that this is a really difficult group to manage. Why don't you work with seniors instead?"

I shrugged and told them that it was precisely because there weren't people working with that age group that we needed to. Especially while they still had two years left in high school to motivate themselves and their classmates before moving on.

After consulting with some friends and people experienced in working with youth, I founded HOBY (Hugh O'Brian Youth). I wanted to target high school sophomores so that they would have two years left in high school to take advantage of what they learned from their HOBY experience. I focused on tenth-graders because when I was a sophomore in high school, at fifteen years of age, I personally had to decide whether I was going to fish or cut bait. There were only two more years of fun and games and then the old, tough world was on top of you.

Fifteen is a very formative age, and I knew it was very important to motivate the students to become aware and excited about what it means to be a US citizen. At fifteen, kids are exploring their identities, wondering who they are as individuals, and thinking about their place in the world community. After the tenth grade, you only have two years left in high school to focus on what you want to do in life, whether you will go on to college or find a job experience in whatever field you want to enter.

The format I wanted for HOBY was not to lecture students with speeches, but to have question-and-answer forums, which is the format HOBY still has today. I wanted to apply what Schweitzer had told me about getting youth to "think for themselves." I didn't want to tell young people what to think, but *how* to think—what the thinking process is all about. I wanted them to be able to make up their own minds, to critically assess

Chapter Eight — **Hugh O'Brian Youth Leadership (HOBY)**

Hugh with HOBY ambassadors, 2005

the world they lived in, to learn how to approach and solve problems and strategize for their future careers.

HOBY is all about getting youth to really understand that their future—and the future of their country—depends on them. I wanted them to be able to identify the problems in their world of today and think of the solutions they would require for the future. In this way, youth would become empowered and learn to believe in themselves. They would realize that the "magic genies" in the world did exist—they existed inside each one of these young people. Youth need to be given the opportunity to explore their thoughts and their future with the guidance of experts; of older, wiser, more experienced adults.

First on my list were the Jaycees because I had just been named one of their "Ten Outstanding Young Men" of the year. I phoned the Santa Monica Jaycees and asked to meet with them. A few days later we met and I explained to them the idea that would eventually become HOBY. I asked these Jaycees to be the first hosts of the program, which we would launch with tenth-graders from about sixty-five local high schools in the central California area.

We planned to put experts on the panel to discuss everything from the future of real estate to what it means to be an American citizen to their responsibilities as young adults. HOBY spread quickly to all fifty states.

HOBY has over four thousand volunteers annually who show teenagers why they should love this country and its incentive system, and love their future lives. In September and October of every year, HOBY nomination material is provided to every public and private high school in the United States, and then it's up to the high school to have the HOBY leadership nomination material available to all their tenth-graders. There is no cost to the students selected to represent their schools.

Students are encouraged to attend local HOBY programs held in every State— about three to four days in length— which

Chapter Eight — Hugh O'Brian Youth Leadership (HOBY)

include leadership building activities and community service projects. They consist primarily of two-hour question-and-answer sessions with panels of three to six experts on the subject. All of our Q and A panels make sure to feature a variety of speakers, people who have been successful in their fields and love to share their experiences. We always focus on having women speakers and minorities. Then, at the conclusion of each program, the local HOBY seminar committee selects a boy and a girl to represent that part of the State at our annual HOBY World Leadership Congress (WLC), which is held in July each year. Each State has at least one HOBY seminar, and the bigger States hold three to five. For instance, Texas and California have five sites. The annual World Congress is coordinated by a major university in a major city. The World Leadership Congress is HOBY's Super Bowl!

When you think about the options kids have these days to spend their time, you can see that the seven-day HOBY World Leadership Congress is pretty remarkable. Working toward something like the HOBY experience has a more lasting meaning than playing a videogame or chatting up with your friends on the Internet!

Well-known entrepreneurs such as Don Tocco, the founder of D.L. Tocco & Associates, a national marketing company, have served as wonderful speakers for HOBY. Tocco Taco, as we call him, has been one of my good friends for many years, and the kids at HOBY have always gravitated toward his energy. Once, some of the kids bought ten-dollar watches from the street vendors in Washington, D.C., and then turned around and sold them to Don for a hundred dollars apiece. We all got a big kick out of the kids' entrepreneurial mindsets and their philanthropic spirit, because they then donated their profits to HOBY!

Through HOBY, I have had the pleasure of meeting other key figures such as astronauts John Glenn, Neil Armstrong, and Buzz Aldrin, who was the captain pilot on *Apollo 11*, which led the first manned landing on the moon. He was the man that Neil Armstrong answered to on the space shuttle. Buzz Aldrin now only lives about five or six miles away from me and has become a good friend.

With Buzz Aldrin (left) and actor Hal Linden

When our first space shuttle, *Apollo 11*, launched, we were fortunate enough to be holding our HOBY World Leadership Congress right there in Cape Canaveral to watch the launch from the Kennedy Space Center. I made three trips to Cape Canaveral a few weeks before the students arrived from all over the world so that I could line up the various programs that we would do and arrange the week so that we could catch the actual launch. These trips and my hard work really paid off!

Hugh at Liftoff

Chapter Eight — **Hugh O'Brian Youth Leadership (HOBY)**

Interestingly enough, one of the fifteen-year-olds who was selected to represent his high school and State at that World Leadership Congress, and still talks about it to this day, was none other than Mike Huckabee, the former governor of Arkansas. A few years ago, Mike Huckabee returned as a speaker at our HOBY World Leadership Congress, and he even got up and performed with the band during our final banquet.

Today, the only kids who make the news are the ones committing crimes or getting into trouble. How come newspapers don't write about the good things kids do? I'd like to see positive kids make the news, too—to show the world how they can give back to the community and make the world a better place to live in.

We've been very successful in getting HOBY Alumni to give over two hundred hours of community service a year, and our goal is always the empowerment of the individual.

Over the years we've had many countries participate in the HOBY World Congress, including Russia, Germany, the United Kingdom, China, Japan, Canada, Korea, Argentina, Chile, and Mexico; they all sent their top tenth-graders. Several years ago, we also had our first group of young leaders from Iraq: five boys and five girls. They've been teaching English there. We were delighted to learn that three of our alumni were there in Iraq as part of the Coalition Provisional Authority, and they decided to hold HOBY motivational programs at two hundred twenty high schools within a two hundred-mile radius of Baghdad.

One of the women who volunteered to assist at the HOBY WLC was a teacher from Iraq and she was kidnapped in her country. Five days later, she was strangled. We were heartbroken to hear the news, but the kids were amazing. They wanted to work even harder, to create a world in which that sort of thing happens less and less until finally, one day, it will no longer happen at all.

In the summer of 2012, Loyola University hosted our HOBY World Leadership Congress in Chicago. Chicago is another great city with a rich and fascinating history. It too has a lot to offer and is a city that everyone should visit at least once. I am proud to say I was raised in Chicago.

Of course, at the end of the day, the place where the HOBY congress is held is not what's important. What is priceless is what happens at the HOBY seminars, in the brainstorming sessions, in the private conversations between these promising future leaders as ideas for the future are bounced around. Each student is encouraged to start thinking about their future and possibilities, and the countless ways their future can and will affect the futures of other human beings, as well as the future of our great country in the World Community. The real magic is what happens inside the mind and heart of each young person. And that's been the most magical return for me.

A lot of people want to know if I get paid for my work with HOBY. The short answer is, No. I don't take a single penny from the organization except in the past for the occasional travel expense. But the real answer is I do get paid—in a phenomenal way, in fact. I get to see the success of these young people who go through our program and who are instrumental in helping HOBY grow. But in order for us to really utilize this, it is very important to keep in touch with our young HOBY participants.

So here's what I say to our HOBY tenth-graders who go through our HOBY program: "You have had this incredible opportunity, one that will possibly change your life. Now you must do something about it. First, you have to give back to your high school and to your community. And second, you must keep in touch with each other. Every year, on your birthday, you owe me a letter—one letter each year, at least until you turn thirty, telling me where you are and what you're into."

Chapter Eight — **Hugh O'Brian Youth Leadership (HOBY)**

These days I average about thirty-five to forty thousand letters each year. I read each one and I try to write back to as many as possible. These letters are my compensation and my reward.

We live in a country where "freedom of speech" and "freedom of choice" are something we talk about a lot and stress in our youth. When you look at our HOBY alumni, you really see the truth of this concept. In America, we truly have the freedom to choose who we want to be and where we want to be.

The young, future leaders that go through our program go on to do great things. About 99.9 percent of them graduate from college and a great many go on to get their doctorates. As far as television goes, a senior VP for daytime programming at NBC was one of my kids. As I mentioned earlier, the former governor of Arkansas, Mike Huckabee, is also one of my kids. There are typically a hundred or more HOBY alums on Capitol Hill at any given time, and over a dozen usually end up serving in the White House. Plus, we have over four hundred and fifty alumni serving with the Department of State all over the world. And did you know that ten to fifteen percent of the top executives of every Fortune 500 company is made up of HOBY alumni?

Now that HOBY has been running for over fifty years, it's amazing to see that the first guys and gals who attended the program are now in their late sixties. When we first got them, they were just kids and now they're focusing on retirement!

But what really excites me is when I think about how each of our HOBY alumni comes into contact with countless youth indirectly, through interviews that some young person might watch on TV or read about in a magazine. Those young people that HOBY alumni meet would become inspired and would think to themselves: "I want to become great and make a difference in the world." And when those young people in turn make something of their lives, they will touch the lives of future youth of the world in a similar fashion.

You can never really predict how much of an impact you will have on the world when you set out to carry out your vision. I now see that the ripple effect from that first trip with Albert Schweitzer has been fantastic.

The success of the Wyatt Earp TV series changed my life and steered me in directions I didn't originally anticipate. For example, playing Wyatt Earp gave me great clout when I wanted to contact the CEOs of Fortune 500 companies such as Johnson & Johnson and General Motors to talk about the purpose of HOBY, and why they should support it. Because of my own experience, I knew how chance meetings and conversations, followed by dedicated effort, played a role in determining our fate. I know that investing in youth through HOBY is a worthwhile endeavor. The personal rewards are priceless and the true benefit to society never can be fully imagined. I have been honored to have great leaders, such as Mikhail Gorbachev, Colin Powell, Larry King, and Katie Couric, as honorees at our annual Albert Schweitzer Leadership Awards (ASLA) dinners for HOBY.

It frustrates me that more people in show business don't use their celebrity to do charitable work and to invest in their communities. Many of them do, but not too many will take the time and expend the energy to create, produce and pay for a program the way I did for HOBY. In our society, the value of a celebrity's name is a high price. One appearance by a famous actor can help an organization break a fundraising record. If all celebrities could understand the weight they have in society and used that knowledge to make a difference, we really could change our country, if not the world.

I love this country, and one of my main purposes for founding HOBY was to teach the next generation of leaders to appreciate our country and care for it the way I do. When you open your newspaper or turn on the TV, you will learn about all of the violence and agony people all over the world experience trying to get some of the basic things we in the United States take for granted—things like freedom and justice. There are people fighting and dying at the hands of tyrants all in search of "freedom of choice"—the ability to choose how their lives will turn out. But even when they do get this freedom, they may not have the resources to really make their dreams a reality. My whole thrust in founding HOBY was to reach out and put my arms around tomorrow, which is what these tenth-graders represent.

When I first began the HOBY program, I had a tenacious drive. I didn't take "no" for an answer. If a sponsor turned me down, I would say, "Okay. But at least sponsor a meal." I used my fame as Wyatt Earp to attract people to HOBY, and it's nice now to meet parents and grandparents who recognize me from those old television shows, but also to meet new HOBY alumni, who simply know me as the guy who started the organization. Both things give me a great deal of satisfaction, but in different ways. On the one hand, there is something incredibly special about being part of someone's past, even just as a television character they loved. On the other, there is something magical—thrilling—about helping to shape someone's future. And that's really what HOBY is all about, and where all my bucks and time have gone.

My work with HOBY and other charities gives me a magnificent way to embrace tomorrow. It's a lot of work, but I've always had fun putting it together, especially because it gives me renewed energy. HOBY is also one key way for me to stay active in retirement. It allows me to reach out in a very cost-effective way, in a very realistic way, in a very giving way, which has a tremendous return by establishing this program, which currently has over 425,000 alumni (and growing). The HOBY organization is respected worldwide.

A lot of kids nowadays don't have the kinds of support that they did when I was growing up. Families are different now. Many kids today grow up in broken or abusive homes. Even the ones who grow up with two parents often don't see Mom and

Dad all that much because the demands of modern life—what with mortgages and car loans and college tuition—often require that both parents work, and work long hours.

The kinds of heroes kids have these days are also quite different, which means a lot of kids are growing up without the right values and the right guidance. There are a lot of negative messages out there and a great deal of cynicism. Our youth are absorbing all of this and it hurts their futures, as well as our nation's future.

I hope HOBY will continue to do what it can to counter those negative influences, and to give kids positive role models to look up to. To further that aim, we offer scholarships and all kinds of resources to students, and we constantly look for ways to adapt to the changing times. It's rewarding to know that the HOBY program I created will exist and thrive, long after I'm gone.

Chapter Nine

Messages from World Leaders

I've had the honor of communicating with a large number of prominent people—from entrepreneurs to the top executives at Fortune 500 companies to US Presidents. I cherish every experience and every conversation with each of these people because their words, wisdom and input over the years have shaped my endeavors—especially HOBY—and have also shaped the man that I am proud to be. In this chapter, I've included a few excerpts of the messages from some of the world leaders who have touched me and have influenced my philanthropy.

Ronald Reagan, 40th President of the United States, and First Lady Nancy Reagan:

"The work of Hugh O'Brian's youth program is an important factor in motivating future leaders to become full participants in our democratic process. Hugh's leadership provides hope—hope for the future of our youth and our nation. Our deep appreciation goes to Hugh for his great and noble efforts."

Norman R. Augustine, Former Chairman and CEO, Lockheed Martin Corp.
"Hugh O'Brian's youth program HOBY has continuously responded to societal changes over 50 years, ensuring its ability to inspire young men and women so that they, in turn, may make positive contributions to their communities. Through Hugh's programs, young people are given an extraordinary opportunity to prepare to become the leaders of tomorrow."

Walter Cronkite, Award-Winning Journalist, CBS News
"Perhaps most importantly, Hugh O'Brian's focus on youth has created a vehicle by which tomorrow's leaders can interact with one another and with today's leaders in learning more about themselves and the institutions which they will shape in future years."

Dr. Malcolm Gillis, President of Rice University, Houston, Texas
"An extraordinary high proportion of participants have gone on to leadership positions in business, government and education. This is just one of the reasons leading colleges and universities take special notice of student applications that feature their Hugh O'Brian leadership participation."

George H. W. Bush, 41st President of the United States, and First Lady Barbara Bush
"Hugh O'Brian's youth program HOBY—and its countless volunteers—has developed a way to educate America's next generation in the art and purpose of leading a free people, and that is an enduring and significant achievement."

Chapter Nine — **Messages from World Leaders**   143

With President George Bush

With First Lady Barbara Bush (left) and TV journalist Barbara Walters

George W. Bush, 43rd President of the United States
"Education plays an essential role in helpings students develop into future leaders. Through these interactive seminars, held annually in each of our United States, Hugh O'Brian's program provides excellent opportunities for students to better understand the working of democracy and our free enterprise system."

Hillary Rodham Clinton, US Secretary of State
"By encouraging leadership and educating teenagers about the vast world of opportunities before them, Hugh O'Brian's outstanding programs for youth are a major contribution to our nation's future."

Ted Turner, Chairman, Turner Broadcasting Systems
"You know, we business people like to say we're driven by the bottom line. The real bottom line is the future, and we owe it to our youth to prepare them for that. Hugh O'Brian does just that by promoting leadership. Hugh is building a corps of young people who will be prepared to meet the challenges facing future generations."

Al Gore, Former Vice-President of the United States, and Tipper Gore
"The continued vitality of American business, our communities and our nation is highly dependent upon the knowledge and capabilities of our young people. Hugh O'Brian's youth programs nurture today's young people into tomorrow's leaders."

Elizabeth Dole, Former US Senator, North Carolina
"Our country has some big and exciting challenges ahead, with some tough choices. Hugh O'Brian's leadership offers a program for our youth to prepare for these challenges and present them with the opportunity to put their stamp on history."

Chapter Nine — **Messages from World Leaders**   145

Hugh with Hillary Rodham Clinton, automobile executive Red Poling, businessman and philanthropist Ted Turner, and student HOBY leaders

With Tipper Gore

Mikhail Gorbachev, Former President of the Soviet Union

"Perhaps all of us—politicians, scholars and public opinion makers—have not yet fully realized one simple fact. It is that we are not just standing on the threshold of a new century but are present at, and participating in, a change of epochs. Hugh O'Brian's youth programs are helping to facilitate that change."

J. Willard Marriot, Jr., Chairman and CEO, Marriot Int'l, Inc.

"Developing and inspiring our nation's youth who will shape the achievements of a new century is critical to all of us. We are proud to support and advance the ideas of Hugh O'Brian's youth leadership program as a means of achieving this worthy goal."

Colin L. Powell, Former US Secretary of State

"The mission of America's Promise is to equip the next generation of Americans with the character and competence they need to be successful adults. Hugh O'Brian is one of our staunch allies in this crusade. He is encouraging each of the thousands of high school sophomores who attend his leadership seminars each spring to volunteer at least a hundred hours a year to a community service project. Hugh's commitment to America's Promise will produce at least 1,400,000 volunteer service hours a year."

Dr. Henry Kissinger, Former US Secretary of State

"World peace can only benefit from future leaders who have the ability to communicate their wisdom and understanding. Hugh O'Brian's outstanding youth program offers these 15-year-old 10th graders the opportunity to expand their horizons by increasing the knowledge of the world they live in, through interaction with today's leaders."

Chapter Nine — **Messages from World Leaders**   147

With General Colin Powell

With Henry Kissinger

James Van Der Beek, Actor and 1993 Alumnus
"One of the best things that Hugh O'Brian's program does is it labels every student who attends the conference as a leader, whether they've ever considered themselves one before or not. Second thing it does is it allows 10th graders, possibly for the first time in their lives, a chance to leave behind everyone else's ideas of who they are. For those very interactive days…they're completely free to come up with their own definition of self…"

Muhammad Ali, Olympic Gold Medalist and World Heavyweight Boxing Champion
"Hugh O'Brian's youth organization is the GREATEST in developing confidence in outstanding students selected annually to represent over 13,500 public and private high schools at one of Hugh's leadership seminars that take place in each of our United States. Hugh O'Brian—What an outstanding role model for our future."

Reverend Billy Graham
"Thank you for bringing me up-to-date on what 'Wyatt Earp' had committed his life to. You are exactly right, no matter who we are, we all have the 'freedom to choose' in our great country. Hugh, I commend you for your vision and the tremendous job you are doing to inspire 10th graders. Keep up your great work!"

Rhena Schweitzer Miller, Daughter of Dr. Albert Schweitzer
"I am very impressed to learn that more than 375,000 young people have now had the benefit of attending your leadership programs which, as I have heard from many, deeply influenced their lives. I don't think you realized the extent or consequences your 1958 visit to my father, Albert Schweitzer, and his talks with you at his hospital in the African forest would have on your

Chapter Nine — **Messages from World Leaders** 149

With Muhammad Ali

With the Reverend Billy Graham

life, and countless others you have touched in his spirit. His words, 'Hugh, what are you going to do with this?,' which he asked you upon your departure, brought about a complete change in your life. My father enjoyed the time you spent together and was very proud to know that he gave you the inspiration to start your youth leadership program. I am grateful that you are still keeping the dream alive over 50 years later, passing on his gift to young people searching for purpose in their lives. I send you my sincere thanks for giving life to my father's inspiration. I am deeply beholden for what you are doing for the youth of the world in his memory."

With Rhena Schweitzer Miller

Chapter Nine — **Messages from World Leaders**

Dr. Gerald Tirozzi, Executive Director, National Association of Secondary School Principals (NASSP)

"Hugh O'Brian's organization HOBY continues to be a vital program serving our youth. NASSP has enjoyed a professional relationship with Hugh since 1972. We believe that the long history and Hugh's commitment are most worthy of our support, as he continues to contribute effectively to the development of tomorrow's leaders today. Hugh O'Brian has my full support and personal endorsement."

Mike Huckabee, Former Governor, State of Arkansas, and 1971 HOBY Alumnus

From a letter I received:

"Dear Mr. O'Brian,

It was a pleasure to talk with you recently by phone and renew the friendship almost 28 years after attending one of your early seminars. The Hugh O'Brian Youth Leadership (HOBY) 1971 Space Seminar at Cape Kennedy was life-changing for me. It was the first time I had traveled outside my home state, my first time to fly on a plane and the first time to meet people from so many diverse places and cultures. I was never the same after that.

The impact of the HOBY seminar on my life was immeasurable. I'm certain that had I not had that experience, I would not have become the governor of my state.

To let you in on some of the trails leading to the present, I'm sending you a copy of a book I wrote called *Character is the Issue*, published in 1997, and a copy of my book *Kids Who Kill*, about the all-too-familiar nightmare of students killing fellow-students in the classroom.

As I mentioned on the phone, I volunteered to meet with some of the local HOBY leaders. I would be most happy to tell of the value of the experience if someone thought it could be of benefit.

Thanks for all you have done for me and thousands of other HOBY "ambassadors."

With every best wish, I am,
Sincerely yours,
Mike Huckabee

PART V

WHO IS HUGH O'BRIAN?

Chapter Ten

Staying Active

In 1993, I stepped down as CEO of HOBY, although I still went into the office almost every day to make solicitation calls, write letters, and ask for donations. After thirty-five years, it was time to let the board take over. But my work with the HOBY organization was far from finished. Now I devote much of my time to philanthropy and fundraising. These days my job is to show the chairmen of the board and the heads of large corporations the value of embracing the future this fifteen-year-old age group represents. These are incredible guys and gals who are our future leaders in business, education, government, full of questions and fresh ideas and unlimited potential, and who still have at least two years left in high school to motivate themselves and their classmates.

Admittedly, I have pursued this job—this passion—at some cost to my so-called acting career. Westerns all but disappeared for years. So did I, when my work was largely reduced to occasional TV walk-ons and touring with road companies and doing Broadway productions. On the one hand, maybe I should have done one show right after another when I was hot and made the big money. On the other hand, I had never started out to be

With President Gerald Ford and HOBY ambassadors at the White House

an actor in the first place. So much for Yale law school, right? I often wonder today where I would have wound up if I had become a lawyer.

But even with all my success in motion pictures, television, and Broadway, and even after I felt I'd mastered my craft across the spectrum of show business, I have never lost sight of the civic and philanthropic opportunities that so-called "stardom" offers to those who are willing to use their popularity and time to motivate others for a worthy cause. I have enjoyed reinvesting my good fortune in many ways to help others, working tirelessly and happily to develop projects to benefit young people around the world during my years of so-called "retirement."

I have a bone to pick with that word, retirement. To me, the word "retire" implies some sort of withdrawal or retreat. It's like in the old Westerns, when the bad guy would retire to his hideout until things cooled off. I may be eighty-nine years old, soon to be ninety, but I'm as active as ever! In my opinion, that's the only way to stay alive: Stay tuned in and actively involved.

If you are contemplating retirement and are hoping to stay mentally active, my advice about planning for it is this: Start to focus at least ten years before then. A lot of people wait to plan until they're nearly or already retired, but there are so many wonderful things you can get involved in as you approach the traditional retirement age. Explore the many different areas or businesses or whatever motivates you. Just make sure you find places where you can be active on many levels. You might even involve yourself in something completely new, something you've never done before, such as nonprofit work, and it just might become a new passion in your twilight years. Then you *really* have something you can enjoy and put your energy into when you get to be that age! Stay productive.

I'm walking proof that it's possible to continue being active when you retire from your so-called business or monetary life—whatever you want to call it. I guarantee you that staying active will exercise the brain and will help you to live an extra ten to twenty years. Because of my involvement with a number of philanthropic causes, I go to sleep at night putting down the last paper or whatever it is, and when I wake up in the morning, there are maybe ten or twenty faxes and emails and things that have come in to go over. It's very invigorating. You don't ever sit there and think, "Oh, what am I going to *do* today?" Or "Gee whiz, honey, when you go to the store, can I please go with you so I feel like I'm *doing* something?"

If you want a really good exercise in every sense of the word, this is one of my favorites. It's a terrific exercise, both physical and mental. Go to a 99-cent store, and then go to Costco or Staples, or vice versa. It's amazing what you'll want to pick up and bring home. There are so many gadgets, gizmos, and other exciting finds that you will always feel like you are leaving with a piece of treasure. Of course, my wife, Virginia, doesn't agree as she's the one who has to unpack and put away all my treasures (crap)!

I also love to send friends a prescription to *Investors' Business Daily*. I know it's actually called a subscription, but I call it a prescription because it's just what the doctor ordered! I just sent a bunch of gifts to friends in the form of annual subscriptions to *National Geographic*. If you've never seen the books that *National Geographic* puts out in addition to the magazine, I strongly suggest you look into them. They're fantastic. And those are things that people just don't expect to get. It's fun doing things like that. It keeps my mind active, always thinking of clever little ways to surprise my friends, and it keeps me happy too, knowing that I am making somebody else happy. Once a month, when they read the latest deep-sea exploration, or dinosaur discovery article in *National Geographic*, I know they are smiling.

Humans have such incredible capacity…for almost anything. Our possibilities and our potentials are astounding, aren't they? Because of the work I've done for the last sixty years, I believe that the world's youth are obviously our future and they are undoubtedly the wisest investment we can make. As Dr. Schweitzer told me in his infinite wisdom, "The most important thing in education is to teach young people to think for themselves." Those words have stuck with me and became a large part of my motivation and way of thinking. They were certainly fundamental in the foundation of HOBY over sixty years ago.

It's been a great honor to receive a number of honorary doctorates over the years because of my philanthropic work. Some have come from very prestigious and well-known institutions that wanted to honor me for the outstanding work I have undertaken on behalf of youth throughout America and the world. These things came my way because of my involvement and participation. And, of course, some of them go way beyond just the metal frame and the certificate. Being the youngest Drill

Instructor in the history of the Marine Corps (USMC) at age seventeen is still one of the things I'm most proud of.

Have you ever heard Marines yell "Ooouu-rahhhh!"? Well, I started that chant. When I was a Drill Instructor, I told my men, "You're really going to hate me when we get through here. The more you hate me the better chance we have to become the Honor Platoon of the eight platoons going through "Boot" at the same time. You get three potty breaks a day, but I do need to know when you go and when you get up, I want you to shout 'Ooouu-rahhhh!'" (I bet Al Pacino didn't know I'd given him his signature line in *Scent of a Woman*! That's not the kind of thing you can hang on a wall.) Well, I'm very proud to have had four of the final platoons I took through "Boot" become the Number One Honor Platoon.

Some of the awards I hold *are* tangible things with real and deeply personal significance for me. "Humanitarian of the Year" award from Lions Clubs International was given to me at the International Convention in Japan in 2002, and with that award came two hundred thousand dollars…which was pretty damn good! I immediately donated that money directly to HOBY—every last penny of it. I have the Jaycees' award for "Outstanding Young Man of the Year" among my most prized possessions.

A lot of the awards are really rewards. They mean a lot to me. Some of them mean more than words can say. For instance, the highest honor that Rotary gives is the Paul Harris Award (Paul Harris was Rotary's founder). Rotary has an unbelievable presence, not just in the United States but around the world. It's in nearly every country and represents a very sizable positive volunteer executive workforce. Rotary is made up of the movers and shakers who run businesses all over the world. But it's also the people who are running colleges that are members of Rotary. Different kinds of businesses and occupations are members of Rotary. I am very proud that they featured me in an article on "Upfront" page in their March 2011 issue of their international publication *The Rotarian*, and you just can't buy that. It's such an extraordinarily beautiful way of saying thank you. And every single time I look at it, I think to myself, "Wow! What an honor this is!"

In 1972, I was awarded one of our nation's highest honors, the "Freedom through Knowledge" Award, sponsored by the National Space Club in association with NASA (National Aeronautics and Space Administration).

In 1973, I was honored by the American Academy of Achievement with their Golden Plate Award.

In 1974, I was awarded the George Washington Medal of Honor, highest award of the Freedom Foundation at Valley Forge, as well as the Globe and Anchor Award from the Marine Corps— highest USMC award.

In 1976, the Veterans of Foreign Wars honored me with the American Patriotic Award.

I am the recipient of the AMVETS Silver Helmet Award, and in 1983, the National Society of Fund Raising Executives (NSFRE) honored me with their Premièr Award for overall Excellence as a volunteer, fundraiser and philanthropist—the only time one individual has received the award in all three categories.

Notre Dame honored me with the first "Pat O'Brien Memorial Award" in 1984. That same year, the Family Counseling Service honored me with its first National Family of Man Award.

In 1989, I received the 60th Annual American Education Award presented by the American Association of School Administrators (AASA). This award is the oldest and most prestigious award that the education profession bestows. I'm very proud to have joined Norman Rockwell, Lyndon Johnson, Helen Keller, Walt Disney, and Bob Hope as a recipient of this most significant award. And the list goes on.

Chapter Ten — **Staying Active**

I don't list my awards to brag or to point to how great I am. I'm *not* great. I've been lucky to work for some great causes and with some great people. And those experiences continue to give my life so much more meaning than it would have otherwise. Actually, the respect I have received for my community work means much more to me than any accolades I ever got for the great career I've enjoyed in "show biz."

You might be thinking, "Can that be true?" Oh, yes! It's not a return I got paid for. And I think it's a wonderful pat on the back. I mean, who wouldn't be proud of that? Especially when you consider what they've brought me in terms of the endless opportunities. I have spoken to Rotary, Lions, Kiwanis, Optimists, General Federation of Women's Clubs, Chambers of Commerce, throughout the world. There's no place I can go where there isn't some basic tie into HOBY. So it's kind of a great return on my investment.

These final days I am very proud of being able to help out in whatever way I can—not only physically, but also mentally. If I can lend my so-called "name" to a project that is doing good work in the world, great. Sign me up. This has helped a tremendous amount to promote events, to bring in money, or to sell tickets to charity events—just by using my name.

We used to put on the Albert Schweitzer Awards dinner for HOBY every year in New York and in Los Angeles. That event—depending on who was being honored—brought in thousands and thousands of dollars to the HOBY organization. It takes a lot of work and an awful lot of marketing. But marketing turns out to be one of the things I think I do pretty well. The reason is not just because I'm vocal or because I think in terms of what's going to happen to any given project, but because of the doors that show business can open for you to call and request support. Fortunately, HOBY's wonderful new leadership and Board of Trustees are once again putting on the ASLA dinner in New York and L.A. every year.

There are a lot of people with strong influence, good common sense, and business acumen who are more willing to help because they know who you are or because they want to know you personally. It's much easier to pick up the phone and talk to the person in charge when you have so-called "name" recognition, so I use it to gain access to a lot of influential people and *also* to encourage their input. This makes a big difference. Example: Hillary Rodham Clinton has raved about our outstanding curriculum for youth, saying that by "encouraging leadership and educating teenagers about the vast world of opportunities before them, these HOBY programs are a major contribution to our nation's future."

I have chosen to use my marketing skills and my recognizable face and name to promote positive youth programs and our great country's future in "The Worlds Committee." A great responsibility, sure, but it has been a great power. And still, even today, I can pick up a phone and call one of the Fortune 500 companies and at least eighty percent of the time be able to get the chairman of the board on the phone—which often elicits a "What the hell does Wyatt Earp want with me?" It's tough for me to take "no" for an answer, and this asset has contributed greatly to HOBY's great success. Call it courage or call it stupidity—whatever it is, my tenacity works!

Not many people can get well-known leaders to show up at a benefit event. It takes supernatural tenacity to persist long enough to corner someone like Colin Powell in an elevator before he'll finally relent and say, "All right, I give up. What do you want?" Katie Couric was also not an easy person to convince to be an honoree at one of HOBY's fundraising dinners, but even she finally agreed because she realized that I wouldn't stop calling until she said yes. Having used my own name to reach as many people as possible, I understood the power that these leaders held and the crowds they could draw. So I made sure to contact all the current "wheels" I could think of. Even General

H. Norman Schwarzkopf finally agreed to be an honoree after his succeess in Operation Desert Storm.

I became well-known for making numerous phone calls to the same person, leaving messages on all their voicemails—home, office, cell until I got a call back. Whenever somebody complains about the number of calls I make to them, my wife, Virginia, says, "I gotcha beat! I get twenty calls a day! So quit your whining! You'll miss them one day, and at least you can have a good laugh after Hugh's gone."

Today, of course, we have something you didn't have way back when—something that's unbelievable in its reach. And that is the website. Now you can visit the Hugh O'Brian Youth Leadership's website, HOBY.org, and even become involved in our local state seminars or our World Leadership Congress through this site. And with the development of social networking websites, the possibilities have continued to expand and grow. Simply being out there on the Internet—and now having these thousands and thousands of people who have become wonderful friends of mine on Facebook—is just incredible. I don't know if young people today can really appreciate how much freedom and how much exposure those opportunities can give to you. In a positive way, I mean. Of course, it can also give you negative exposure. It really is about what you "do" with it. You can reap what you put into it.

I should mention that even before I founded HOBY, my incredible good fortune in show business gave me the opportunity to 'give back' to the community in some measurable way. In the Fifties I, along with my young, talented fellow-actors, had the image of totally irresponsible entertainers who did nothing but party, marry and divorce. So on Mother's Day in 1955, I pulled together a group to meet at Jayne Mansfield's "Pink Palace" in Beverly Hills to figure out how to change that image. We decided to devote our energy and resources to children with mental health problems. We named our organization "The

Thalians," after the Goddess of Comedy, Thalia. I was elected our first president.

For over fifty years, the organization has raised millions of dollars, thanks to the dedication and hard work of top fundraisers like Stephanie J. Hibler, who has served on the Board of Directors for over forty-eight years and produced many Thalian fundraising events. We established the Thalians Mental Health Center to serve not only children but adults as well. Most recently, we expanded our efforts to partner with UCLA's Operation Mend: Healing America's Returning Soldiers in Mind, Body and Spirit.

Each year, a series of these events have taken place with a Ms. or Mr. Wonderful being honored at a Gala and fabulous entertainment provided. My pal, Hugh Hefner, received the prestigious award at The Thalians 55th Gala in 2011, for his lifetime of philanthropy.

My friend Debbie Reynolds followed me as president, alternating with the wonderful actress Ruta Lee, for fifty-plus years! She and Ruta have always opened the Gala evening with a smashing duet. Both of these incredible women, with hearts of gold, are now Presidents Emeritus but Debbie still serves as Thalians' Chairman of the Board.

So, life as I said, can be what you make it…but often love comes along to make that journey even more rewarding.

It's true that I dated quite a few gals over the years—more than it might be polite to discuss right here with you, as a perfect stranger! But I'll tell you this: I will always remember when Virginia Stumpf*(Barber) and I first met. We were at a dinner party in a restaurant with about twelve other guests and were seated next to each other. By the end of the evening, I had her phone number. And as she always likes to say, "Hugh started

---

* She was married to a Mr. Barber briefly in the early '90s and kept the name for teaching purposes. She no longer uses it.

Chapter Ten — **Staying Active**

The romance blooms

calling me the next day and hasn't stopped." And that was over twenty-five years ago in September of 1988.

Virginia is beautiful in every way. This gorgeous lady was born and raised in Los Angeles, California. She had a beautiful Canadian mother of Norwegian and English descent and a father of German descent from St. Louis, Missouri.

Her family name, Stumpf, and my family name, Krampe, are both German names which gave us somewhat common backgrounds. She makes German potato salad and cooks up sauerkraut and knockwurst and I'm a happy, well-fed man.

When I first met Virginia, she was in the fashion business with a showroom at the California Mart in downtown Los Angeles. She was also traveling to Market Weeks in New York and throughout the Southwest. She was also teaching a class or two in Retail Marketing and Fashion Merchandising to high school students, and was a public speaker in high schools for her alma mater, FIDM (The Fashion Institute of Design and Merchandising). Needless to say, she was very busy and difficult to keep track of. She was a challenge.

Hugh and Virginia
The perfect wedding day

I knew she was "one-of-a-kind" and I needed to pursue her! Her involvement with teenagers and my involvement with that age group through HOBY gave us even more common ground.

After we had dated a few times, I did the supreme test, which was to take her to Hawaii. She handled the trip very well and I took special notice. I had dated a couple hundred lovely ladies throughout my long bachelorhood, and my romantic past was spotted with all kinds of big names—from Hollywood royalty like Ava Gardner to Princess Soraya of Iran after she divorced the Shah—and all kinds of personalities, including a girlfriend who once showed up at my old house with her pet tiger! But there was something different this time around.

Virginia was the one who proved that she was the right one in every way. She's the finest lady I've ever known. I had waited for her for about forty-five years. There's no way in the world that I could have done any better than this lovely woman who not only puts up with me, but shares her greatest sense of

Chapter Ten — **Staying Active**

humor and is beautiful inside and out. She also just happens to be the world's greatest cook. (Virginia, I LOVE you!)

We were longtime friends who grew comfortable with each other, and then—after eighteen years—she agreed to marry me. The night before I popped the question to Virginia, I wrestled with the possibility that she might turn me down. But I had tested the marketplace for years and I knew that I wanted to have a lifelong relationship with Virginia. That's a rare feeling to have toward someone. So when it comes along, you need to jump on it so that it doesn't get away.

I was eighty years old when I asked her to marry me and eighty-one when we got married. For most of my life I had always wanted a relationship like my mom and dad had, but I've seen too much unhappiness in couples I knew. So many of my friends have gone through their second or third divorces already. But Virginia and I? Well, she's the love of my life. What a perfect pair of newlyweds we were. And what a perfect wedding!

The event, which took place on June 25, 2006, was an unbelievable experience. In line with our theme, "The Wedding to Die For," we vowed "til death do us part' at the Hall of Crucifixion up at the very top of the hill of Forest Lawn in Glendale, California. The beautiful three-hundred-acre property serves as the final resting place to silver screen icons Errol Flynn, Spencer Tracy, Clayton Moore, Jimmy Stewart, Clara Bow, and Humphrey

Hugh and Virginia with wedding guests John Rockwell and Crystal Salapatas, the culprits who introduced us in 1988

Sharing the happy hearse at Forest Lawn

Bogart, just to name a few. I chose this location along with our "The Wedding to Die For" theme because getting married for the first time at my age is unusual. I figured that if anything were to happen to me on our "big day," then nobody would have to come back for the funeral. They could just stick me in the ground right there on the same day!

Many of our beloved friends and family were present. Our good friend and living Hollywood legend Debbie Reynolds sang, "It had to be Hugh. It had to be Hugh" to the melody of the popular Isham Jones song, "It Had to Be You." I was picked up near my home on Mulholland Drive in the very hearse that was featured on *The Munsters*, which I borrowed from George Barris. The wedding featured all kinds of characters including look-alikes who played Pope John Paul II and John Wayne.

Among the two hundred or so wedding guests were friends, loved ones, and also many HOBY volunteers. The ceremony—described by many as bizarre and/or interesting—was conducted by the Reverend Robert Schuller, pastor of the former Crystal

Cathedral in Garden Grove. The memorable event concluded with an equally memorable cocktail reception, where we released a flock of butterflies to Virginia's family, buried nearby Errol Flynn, Clayton Moore (the Lone Ranger), and Spencer Tracy, in the Garden of Everlasting Peace; but most amazing was the generosity of many of our guests, who donated to HOBY in lieu of a gift. Once it was over, we got to ride home on the freeway in the hearse. My lovely bride and I spent our honeymoon taking a philosophy course, "Minds, Robots, and Souls," at England's Oxford University, and touring by car through England. After all, an active mind is as important as an active body and, fortunately, my lady love puts up with me.

When I first began dating Virginia, I certainly wasn't looking for a wife. I had never been married before. But our friendship naturally evolved into a marriage and that was my first—and most definitely my last—trip down the aisle. I know I said it before, but I'll say it again: She is one of the finest ladies I've known. Virginia IS "my life." And I didn't know it at the time,

Ready to drive off in Munsters-style. Thank you, George Barris!

but it turns out that not only is Virginia the best cook in the world but she's also the best hostess! She has thrown great birthday parties for me honoring my stage and film career. For example, we celebrated *Africa-Texas Style!* with guests showing up in African safari attire.

Today, Virginia and I share an extraordinarily beautiful and comfortable Benedict Canyon home with our dog "Cowboy" and our cat "Koko." We often sit on our chaise lounge on our outdoor patio deck and peer out across the canyon and the Pacific Ocean. On a clear day, we can see as far as Catalina Island. Sometimes we'll take our dinner outside and then get under the covers on the double chaise lounge and camp out for the night. When the moon is full and the stars are bright, we enjoy a private and fantastic camping experience right outside our very own home.

Now, in my late eighties, I make it a point to continue experiencing as many adventures as I can and to keep my mind sharp. I will never stop learning, and one of my burning passions is for young people to understand and appreciate the potential power and the curiosity of their brain. I have many friends who've retired and resorted to playing golf once or twice a week and not doing much else. They do nothing to make their minds "buzz." To me, mental exercise is as important as physical exercise—whether it be watching a Lakers basketball game, traveling, reading, or learning a new magic trick.

I keep myself busy all day. My day begins about eight in the morning and then I'm up until eleven o'clock or midnight. I rarely watch television unless Virginia wants me to take a look at something special. In order to keep busy and take care of my incoming and outgoing correspondence, I head to the bedroom after dinner and TV to work into the night. I stay abreast of current events with publications such as the *Los Angeles Times*,

Investors' Business Daily, *The Wall Street Journal*, *Barron's*, and *Time* magazine.

Let me tell you, I am now a champion of the simple necessity of exercising your mind just as much as you exercise your body. A lot of people get to the age where they retire, only to discover that they don't have the type of hobbies that allow them to contribute and truly get something out of contributing. There's only so much golf or tennis they can play as they get older. But keeping the mind active is just as important as physical exercise. Mental exercise is extremely important to having a long number of healthy years to live after you retire before you pass on.

There are just not enough hours in the day for me to do all the projects which, in one way or the other, I'm either running, orchestrating the outcome of, or laying the foundation for. I'm always starting new projects and putting things together. There is always "something." And I wouldn't have it any other way.

I have had the privilege of becoming friends with many of our country's presidents. Eisenhower, Nixon, Carter, Reagan, Clinton, and both presidents Bush. But at my age, you do start to think about those various administrations and how they personally handled things. There wasn't one of them that didn't have an excellent personality. They were very interesting and productive people. I still haven't met the best US President, though. That person is still out there. All these other guys were great—I mean truly great men—but there are a lot of wonderful people out there now that are going to be in a position—who should be in a position—to be one of our "best" presidents, whether it's the next administration or the one after that.

I do think our country is ready for a female president. I think that there is a lot of value in that in terms of showing what this country is and what it can do and what the future might be.

I do very much believe in our democratic process. Our right and "freedom to choose" is one of our greatest heritages and one

With President Nixon

that needs to be protected. If I see something that concerns me or bothers me, then I look into it in depth. Politics has always been and will be an area of interest because of its role in our democratic process. I've been asked to run for office several times in the past, but I won't because I feel I can be more objective on the outside looking in. Besides, I'm knowledgeable but I'm not an expert. If something *does* happen that causes me worry, then I'll focus on what I first need to focus on to understand the situation.

The main reason that I started the Hugh O'Brian Youth Leadership Program is because I care so much about our country and its Free Enterprise System. In realizing, like everybody else,

Chapter Ten — **Staying Active**   173

that it doesn't matter how much money you earn or what kind of successes you have in life; you're not going to live forever. You can't buy tomorrow. Being backed throughout the years by friends and celebrity supporters such as Jimmy Stewart, Walter Cronkite, and Charlton Heston, as well as corporate sponsors around the nation, has been such a blessing, too. I feel very, very strongly about the value of these GREAT United States and what it represents: the "freedom of choice," the true worth of being independent, and not living under any kind of *sword*, or under the shadow of evil.

I've also always hoped and seen that HOBY can and does provide a program for the young people of today, the ones who will be running our great country tomorrow. I believe that HOBY alumni are and will be the key leadership, running the Fortune 500 companies and our government. Many of the other business representatives of HOBY have influenced our country in a variety of ways—the educational system, our democratic process, big business, government, and so on. The volunteers who help make this happen are such unbelievably great examples of what volunteerism is and what it means to this country of ours.

And, you know that famous *Life* magazine cover photo of a gal being kissed by a sailor in Times Square celebrating the end of World War II? Well, the woman in the photograph was Edith Shain, and I had the pleasure of working with her on a project, "The Spirit of '45." She was just the sweetest woman and it was an honor to meet her. The connections I have made in life are so many and so meaningful. There is just no way to put a price on the terrific leaders and "doers" who have embraced my vision—I couldn't begin to try.

With all these efforts, all the connections and friends and partners, our ongoing youth programs, and everything in-between, I feel we have really come full circle and will continue to get the message out there, "move forward boldly, plan for a strong positive future, and continue to develop and evolve." We have made a name for ourselves. It is important to take that notoriety and put it to good use. You don't have to start a youth organization, but if you have your notoriety, *use it*. You can be an effective help to any existing organization. Your future looks fantastic!

Travel is something I've always loved and look forward to. Virginia and I recently took a two-week cruise to Norway to see the gorgeous fjords and to give Virginia a chance to see the country of her ancestors. It truly was a trip of a lifetime. In the future, we'd like to see more of our great United States along with countries we haven't been to together, such as Sweden, Russia, Peru, Belize and/or perhaps a photographic safari in Africa where I filmed a couple of movies.

Virginia is a great travel partner. We've gone salmon fishing on the Kenai River in Alaska, drunk ouzo in the Greek Isles, shopped flea markets in Paris, studied at Oxford in England, experienced the tango in Argentina, walked the Great Wall of China, slept in a longhouse on Borneo, glided in the air over Oahu, Hawaii; drank wine on the Napa Valley, CA wine train, rode horses in Wyoming, and camped out in the hills of Beverly Hills. And, Virginia has driven us on the other side of the road and the other side of the car in England, and we are still alive and laughing.

Chapter Eleven

Pitching for the Ninth Inning

Nobody knows what happens after this final stage in life. You can have your own set of beliefs, which is important, but everything about the afterlife is still conjecture. I really don't know whether there is a hell or a heaven, but I do believe that you can create heaven and hell here on earth. Most of us know that the better you are as a person and the kinder you are, the happier you will be in life.

I don't live my life expecting to make it to heaven. I live it by trying to create a heaven here on earth. Heaven and hell take place all around you, every day. What you contribute to society creates what you get. And if you give back to your community and help others, then what you get back are smiles, laughter, tears of joy and appreciation, and a small heaven here and now for those you touch. I truly believe the greatest gift you will ever receive is the gift you give to someone else.

Sometimes living with any kind of fame or recognition can be a double-edged sword. Certainly there are perks, but there are times when the most desirable option would be to vanish, subtly and silently like vapor—quickly, softly, unseen and unsensed. You work for what you want, you get it, and then suddenly you don't have a moment to yourself. A character—a great character, the prize you've fought so hard for—can be difficult to separate from.

In many ways I feel like I've lived many lives. My four years in the Marine Corps were incredibly different from my time doing live theatre, and my film career was more different still. Another life, then another life, and so on. I kept very busy as I climbed up the ladder. I worked hard and sometimes played harder. That kind of life can be so exhausting. It really does take a lot out of you, paying all those dues, but somehow you've got to do it.

Have you ever seen those old signs that read "No Dogs or Actors Allowed?" A long time ago, they put those signs up in front of hotels and apartments. That left the performers complaining mercilessly about not getting fair billing. The insecurity of the profession has even come through in political campaigns. When Ronald Reagan successfully ran for Governor of California in 1966, one unproductive tactic used by his opposition was a television commercial that featured Gene Kelly saying, "In films I played a gambler, a baseball player, and I could play a Governor...but you wouldn't really want an actor to really be a Governor, would you?"

Plenty of other people have written about the insecurity of actors, so there's no need to dredge it all up here. But I would like to make one thing clear here: I'm NOT an actor and I have many films to prove it.

I do like to tell the story of a lifelong friend of mine named Jake, who loved his German Shepherd Butch. We had been friends since grammar school and one thing we had in common was our love of dogs. Six months after Butch died at the ripe old age of twelve, my dear friend also died.

Several weeks after Jake passed, he started contacting me in my sleep. In the afterlife, the German Shepherd licked Jake's face until he woke up. Neither one of them knew whether they

Chapter Eleven — **Pitching for the Ninth Inning**

were in heaven or hell, but Butch possessed a definite sense of where he wanted to go, so he led his master into the woods. A hundred yards or so in, they found a clearing and an exquisite castle with several gold domes. In front of the castle, a man wearing a tuxedo sat at an ornate desk about ten feet long, so Jake and his dog approached the desk.

"Mr. Jones, as you can see, we've been waiting for you," said the man.

"Where am I?" Jake asked.

"You're in heaven," answered the man. "Please sign our book here and respond to a few questions, and you can go right over the bridge there into the magical castle."

Jake, who was mesmerized by the beautiful surroundings, quickly filled out the form and headed in the direction of the castle with Butch.

"Wait a minute," said the man at the desk. "You can't take your dog."

"What do you mean?" asked Jake.

"Pets aren't allowed in the castle."

"But he's my best friend."

"Sir, NO PETS are allowed!"

So Jones turned to his pal and said, "I don't think we want to go in there. You're my best friend and we stick together."

So Butch turned around and started off in another direction. Jake naturally followed. They walked through the woods for about another forty or fifty yards until they came to yet another clearing, where they saw an old Connecticut-style farmhouse village. There was no fence and the entire environment appeared to be a common home. An old man stood whittling by a tree.

Jake and the dog walked over to the man, who said, "Mr. Jones, we've been waiting for you."

"Where am I?" asked Jake.

The man replied, "This is heaven."

"How can this be heaven when we were just at heaven back there?" asked Jake.

"That wasn't heaven. That's hell. *This* is heaven."

"Well if that's true, why did that place down there claim to be heaven?" he asked.

"To try to get you first. And the people who learn quickly enough that it isn't heaven make it up here."

Jake glanced at the house and then looked at the man and then looked at his four-legged friend and asked, "What about my dog Butch? Can I take him with me?"

And the man said, "He's your best friend. Of course you can take him."

That story tells the difference between one man's heaven and hell.

Heaven is also the place where smart and capable kids grow up to make a difference in their world. I'm sick and tired of reading headlines about kids who have stolen cars, vandalized schools, created disturbances—rebelled in some way or other against society. These kids represent only a tiny part of the teenagers in this country! And I should know, having worked with thousands of these kids. It's a fact that 98.7 percent of our young people are law-abiding, constructive citizens. It's time we accent the positive, pat the good guys and gals on the back. These are the future leaders of the world. STOP giving attention to the BULL!

My personal goal when working with young people—and with people in general—is for each person to realize that as an individual they are totally unique. In this world, there's nobody else like you and you truly have the opportunity to accomplish anything you set your mind to. It may be more difficult for some, but everyone has a chance to succeed in one way or another if they really work at it. So these HOBY alumni become my legacy. I pass on what I have learned to them; they use it, grow, succeed, and pass it on to the next generation. Tomorrow is endless!

Chapter Eleven — **Pitching for the Ninth Inning**

The world we live in is so very large and so unbelievably small all at the same time. There are so many different kinds of people, so many ideas and ways of doing things. When I think of all the people I've met throughout my life, the cross-section is amazing. I don't know that I ever officially retired from acting, but I also don't know that I ever really acted. There are a lot of directors that might agree with that, even though I did five shows on Broadway, was in twenty-nine movies and over four hundred TV shows. But I loved show biz, I enjoyed it… would I do more of it? Sure, if the right role came along, why not? Also, Virginia has never seen me on stage so a play might be fun to do.

As I mentioned earlier in this book, Buddy Hackett and I may have turned down the opportunity to do a series together as a comedic duo, but he and I remained very good friends. Toward the end of Buddy's life, I spoke with him a few times a year, about once every three or four months. The last time we spoke was about two months before he passed away. By then, Buddy had stopped going out and remained inside his house all the time. He no longer played golf. When I said to him, "Buddy, you have to get out of your house," he simply answered, "Why? I've been there! I've seen everything!" That complete inactivity is what eventually killed him. Sure, he had a special interest in guns and rifles, but that's a hobby you can only look at so many times.

When I think of Buddy now, I remember his Viagra joke about not peeing on his shoes anymore. Good ol' Buddy. He is still making me laugh today.

Getting older happens in five stages First there is "Who Is Hugh O'Brian?" Second, there is "Get Me Hugh O'Brian." The third stage is "Get Me a Hugh O'Brian type." The fourth is "Get Me a Young Hugh O'Brian." And the fifth stage is "Who is Hugh O'Brian?" I think it's funny when people say, "Hugh O'Brian is still alive???" Wow!

Life is certainly something to celebrate, and I like to celebrate in style. Birthdays are the perfect time to do that—and my birthday parties are legendary. It's true. My 77th birthday had an elaborate Cinco de Mayo celebration theme, my 78th involved a chili cook-off, and my 79th found numerous guests bellying up to "The Last Chance Saloon."

My 80th birthday was huge, a three-day celebration. The first day began the festivities with a VIP cocktail reception attended by close friends and family in Beverly Hills. On the second day, our guests explored Hollywood and local Los Angeles attractions. The third and last day was my big bash at the Autry Museum of the American West. Not only was it an exciting time, but all of the profits from the event went directly to my HOBY organization.

Coming up with new slogans each year is fun. My 84th birthday rang in the year of, "I'm eighty-four and looking for more." My 85th year was celebrated as, "I'm eight-five and still

Celebrating with Shirley Jones

alive." My 86th was "I'm eighty-six and still getting kicks," and we celebrated my theatre career with a *Music Man* theme.

My "87 and still trying for Heaven" with the African and wild animal theme celebrated all the wild stunts I did in movies like *Africa-Texas Style!* or the other title *Cowboy in Africa*. I'm going to keep having a great time as long as I can. That's important. I live happily with my lovely wife, I keep learning and evolving, and I give back all I can and then some. In fact, this fairly current description of myself might just be my best bio yet: "Mr. O'Brian lives with his beautiful wife, Virginia, in a hilltop home overlooking Beverly Hills. Diverse as ever, his leisure activities include swimming, traveling, and magic." I like it. That's me.

I didn't grow up dreaming of being a movie and television star, nor did I plan to be a philanthropist and humanitarian. I wanted to go to Yale to become a lawyer. But now, when I play a lawyer, I win all my cases and get paid more. How do you like them apples, Perry Mason?

Sometimes life isn't what you think you want, but that's not always a bad thing. It can be so much better than you had ever even dared to imagine. I am proud of the person I've become—a person who cares very much about this great country, our world, and the future of all our young citizens. One of these days I won't be around any longer, but they will. It feels good to know that I'm part of building a tremendous force for the future of our world.

Truthfully, I've never stopped being curious about our universe. I'm curious when I wake up in the morning. I grow more curious during the day; and at night, when I go to bed, I'm still curious. I never get to the end of it. And the many different opportunities out there.

The greatest gift you can give is the positive "light" that you can give to somebody else. Being active in charities is great, but it doesn't stop there. Shine in your lifestyle. Promote a joyful existence. People who live negatively are not generally happy. But I'm pretty happy with my life and have received countless letters. I created HOBY because I've always been very aware that I will not be around forever. I have been very blessed in this lifetime—whether it was by God or by the universe or by simply doing positive things—and the returns I've received for those non-monetary investments I've made are a thousandfold. After I'm gone, I'd like the returns to keep on coming to everyone who remains involved in HOBY.

But I'm not done yet! You can't get rid of me that easy. I bet I can *still* do the quick draw faster than anyone can blink, and I am proud to have served as national chairman of the "Spirit of '45" campaign. I hope to continue finding causes that speak to me, and to continue giving back and helping out in any way I can for as long as I can.

I have no regrets about the choices I have made. After all these years, I am still enjoying every moment of life with my dear Virginia, friends, family, and fans by my side. I have chosen to utilize what fame and success I've created for myself to motivate others for a worthy cause, to raise awareness, and to reinvest my good fortune by continually developing projects to benefit young people. My perpetual goal and longtime vision has been to empower individuals and help motivate them to make positive differences within our country, our global society, and the world committee. This can be done through compassion, understanding, and effective, intelligent action based on confident leadership. Most importantly, it works.

If you're going to be successful at something, it will be because you enjoy doing it, so try to find a job that you enjoy doing—one that really makes you want to get up in the morning. It's never too late. You can begin again right now. In the United States especially, you have the freedom to choose to be anything you want to be.

Chapter Eleven — **Pitching for the Ninth Inning**

If there's one philosophy that sums it all up for me, it's right here in my credo:

> **The Freedom to Choose**
>
> I do NOT believe we are all born equal—CREATED equal in the eyes of God, YES—but physical and emotional differences, parental guidance, varying environments, being in the right place at the right time, all play a role in enhancing or limiting an individual's development. But I DO believe every man and woman, if given the opportunity and encouragement to recognize his or her own potential, regardless of background, has the freedom to choose in our world. Will an individual be a taker or a giver in life? Will that person be satisfied merely to exist, or seek a meaningful purpose? Will he or she dare to dream the impossible dream?
>
> I believe every person is created as the steward of his or her own destiny with great power for a specific purpose: to share with others, through service, a reverence for life in a spirit of love.

We ALL have the freedom to choose, and I hope you exercise that freedom to choose well. Dream the impossible dream, my friends, and go after everything you want. Who knows? You just might get it. I'll be eighty-nine on April 19, 2014 and I continue to seek my own heaven every day.

Appendix A

Honorary Doctorates

1986

    Doctor of Humane Letters   St. Mary of the Plains
                                                   Dodge City, Kansas

    Doctor of Humane Letters   Lebanon Valley College
                                                   Annville, Pennsylvania

    Doctor of Laws   St. John's University
                                                   Jamaica, New York

1987

    Doctor of Public Service   University of Denver
                                                   Denver, Colorado

1991

    Doctor of Humane Letters   Bloomsburg University
                                                   Bloomsburg, Pennsylvania

1991

    Doctor of Humane Letters   Green Mountain College
                                                   Poultney, Vermont

2000

    Doctor of Public Service   The George Washington University
                                                   Washington, .D.C.

2003

    Doctor of Fine Arts   Troy State University
                                                   Troy, Alabama

Appendix B

Awards Received

1971	Freedom through Knowledge – National Aeronautics & Space Administration (NASA)
1973	Golden Plate Award – American Academy of Achievement
1974	George Washington Medal of Honor – Freedoms Foundation, Valley Forge
	Globe and Anchor Award – National Marine Corps Scholarship Foundation
1975	American Patriotic Award – Veterans of Foreign Wars (VFW)
1976	Humanitarian Award – District of Columbia
1978	Governor's Award – State of Ohio
1979	Service to Mankind Award – Hollywood Sertoma Club
1980	Silver Helmet Award – AMVETS
1982	Outstanding Support to the Youth of America – U.S. Jaycees
1983	Premier Award for Overall Excellence as a Volunteer Fundraiser and Philanthropist – National Society of Fund Raising Executives (NSFRE)
1984	First Pat O'Brien Memorial Award – University of Notre Dame Club, Chicago
	First National Family of Man Award – Family Counseling Service
1985	Semper Fidelis Award – U.S. Marine Corps
1986	Ambassador Award – U.S. Jaycees
	Outstanding Love & Concern – General Federation of Women's Clubs
1987	American Education Award – American Association of School Administrators
	General William Booth International Humanitarian Award – Salvation Army

Appendix B - Awards Received

	Holiday Project Award – City of San Francisco, California
1989	Education Award (60th Annual) – American Association of School Administrators (AASA)
1990	Lifetime Achievement Award – Los Angeles Business Council
1992	Western Heritage Wrangler Award – Great Western Performers Hall of Fame
1993	Lifetime Achievement Award – The Franklin Mint
	The Real Top Gun Award – HOBY Board of Trustees & Governors
1994	Private Enterprise Exemplar Medal – Freedom Foundation at Valley Forge
	American Celtic Globe Humanitarian – Ireland Chamber of Commerce (ICCUSA)
1995	Foundation Fellow – Ohio District Kiwanis Foundation
	Award of Honor – Hearts at Work
	Vision Award – ESA International (Epsilon Sigma Alpha)
1997	1996 Man of the Year - KNX Newsradio
	Treasures of Los Angeles - Central City Association of L.A. (CCA)
1998	Meritorious Public Service Citation - The United States Department of Navy
2000	Ellis Island Medal of Honor - Nat. Ethnic Coalition of Organizations (NECO)
	Champions of Children - Cystic Fibrosis Foundation
	Lifesaver Award - The Thalians
	Teddy Roosevelt Youth Leadership Award (first given) - Rocky Mountain College
	Certificate of Merit - Freedom's Foundation at Valley Forge
	Lifetime Achievement in Philanthropy - Nat. Society of Fundraising Executives (NSFRE) (First time this award given)
	Angel Award - Blue Cross Blue Shield of Louisiana
2001	Guest of Honor - Marine Corps Sunset Parade

2002 Distinguished Service Award - Nat. Assoc. of Secondary School Principals (NASSP)

Humanitarian Award - Lions Clubs International (This included $200,000, which Hugh generously donated to HOBY)

2006 Excellence in Education - National Assoc. for College Admission Counseling (NACAC)

2008 Paul Harris Award - Rotary International

2013 The Edson A. Benedict Award - Benedict Canyon Association "Through service, a reverence for life in a spirit of love"

Appendix C

Hugh O'Brian Credits

THEATRE

BROADWAY:

Cactus Flower Directed by Abe Burrows
Destry Rides Again Directed by Michael Kidd
First Love Directed by Alfred Lunt
Guys and Dolls Directed by Jean Darrimple
The Decision Directed by Abe Burrows

REGIONAL:

A Thousand Clowns (3 productions)
Angel Street
Cactus Flower (The National Company)
Desperate Hours
Guys & Dolls (4 productions)
Hamlet
The Hasty Heart (2 productions)
Mr. Roberts (3 productions)
Mourning Becomes Electra
The Music Man (3 productions)
The Odd Couple (2 productions)
Of Mice and Men
Picnic (2 productions)
Plaza Suite (2 productions)
The Rainmaker (3 productions)
Stalag 17
The Tender Trap (2 productions)
20th Century

Appendix D

Hugh O'Brian Credits

MOTION PICTURES

Africa - Texas Style! 1967 Paramount
 (Also released as: Cowboy in Africa)

Ambush Bay 1966, Paramount

Back to God's Country 1953, Universal

Battle at Apache Pass 1952, Universal

Beyond the Purple Hills 1959, Columbia

The Brass Legend 1956, Universal

Broken Lance 1954, 20th Century Fox

Buckaroo Sheriff of Texas 1951, Republic

Cave of the Outlaws 1951, Universal

The Cimarron Kid 1951, Universal

Come Fly with Me 1963, Columbia

The Daltons 1952, Universal

Drums Across the River 1954, Universal

The Fiend Who Walked the West 1958, 20th Century Fox

Fighting U.S. Coast Guard, Republic

Fireman, Save My Child! 1954, Universal

Game of Death 1979, Warner Brothers

In Harm's Way 1965, Warner Brothers

Killer Force 1975

The Lawless Breed 1952, Universal

Little Big Horn 1951, Universal

Love Has Many Faces 1965, Columbia

The Man from the Alamo 1953, Universal

Meet Me at the Fair 1952, Universal

Never Fear 1949, The Filmakers
    (Also released as: The Young Lovers)

On the Loose 1951, The Filmakers

The Raiders 1952, Universal

Red Ball Express 1952, Universal

The Return of Jesse James 1950, Lippert Pictures

Rocketship X-M 1950, Lippert Pictures

Sally and Saint Anne 1952, Universal

Saskatchewan 1954, Universal

Seminole 1953, Universal

The Shootist 1976, Warner Brothers

Son of Ali Baba 1952, Universal

Stand at Apache River 1953, Universal

Ten Little Indians 1966, Paramount

There's No Business Like Show Business 1954, 20th Century Fox

Twinkle in God's Eye 1955, Republic

Twins 1990, Universal

Vengeance Valley 1951, MGM

White Feather 1955, 20th Century Fox

Appendix E

Hugh O'Brian Credits

TELEVISION

The Life and Legend of Wyatt Earp
    1955-1961, ABC (226 Episodes)

Search
    1971-1972, NBC

GUEST STARRING ROLES:

Alfred Hitchcock Presents
    1962, CBS

Bob Hope Presents the Chrysler Theatre
    (4 episodes), NBC

Charlie's Angels
    ABC

Cruise into Terror
    1978, TV Movie of the Week, ABC

Circus of the Stars
    CBS

The Danny Thomas Show
    1956, CBS

Dial M for Murder
    1967, TV Movie, NBC

Dinah Shore Chevy Show
    (2 episodes), NBC

DuMont Royal Theatre/Playhouse
    1951/52, DuMont network

The Ed Sullivan Show
    (4 episodes), CBS

Fantasy Island
    (Pilot & 4 episodes), ABC

Feathertop (Musical Comedy)
    1961, 2-hour NBC Special

Fireside Theatre
    (4 episodes), NBC

General Electric Theatre
    (3 episodes), CBS

The George Gobel Show
    (2 episodes), NBC

The Greatest Show On Earth
    1963, ABC

Gunsmoke II
    1990, TV Movie of the Week

Hallmark Hall of Fame
    (4 episodes), NBC

Harpy
    1971, CBS, 1st two-hour Movie of the Week

Hollywood Palace
    (2 episodes), ABC

It's a Man's World
    2-hour Special

I've Got A Secret
    CBS

The Jackie Gleason Show
    (2 episodes), CBS

Kraft Television Theatre
    (3 episodes), NBC

L.A. Law
    NBC

The Love Boat
    (Pilot & 2 episodes), ABC

The Luck of the Draw: The Gambler Returns
    1991

The Millionaire
    (3 episodes), CBS

Murder on Flight 502
    1975, TV Movie of the Week, ABC

Murder She Wrote
    1990, CBS

Oboler Comedy Theatre
    1949, ABC (first TV show that paid actors)

Paradise
    1990, (2 episodes), CBS

Perry Mason
    1963, CBS (one of four episodes without Raymond Burr)

Password
    1962/1963; CBS

Playhouse 90
    (3 episodes), CBS

Police Story
    (Pilot & 3 episodes), NBC

Probe
    (Pilot for "Search" TV series) 1971

A Punt, A Pass and A Prayer
    Hallmark Hall of Fame, NBC

Sing Out, Sweet Land
    1969, John Wayne Special

Space in the Age of Aquarius
    1969, 2-hour Special (produced & directed by Hugh O'Brian)

Studio 57
    1955, DuMont network

The Virginian
    1962, (Pilot), CBS

Westinghouse Desilu Playhouse
    1959, Christmas Special, CBS

What's My Line?
    1961/1966; CBS

Wild Women
    1970, TV Movie of the Week, ABC

Wyatt Earp: Return to Tombstone
    1994, 2-hour Movie of the Week, CBS

SPECIAL NOTE:

The Life and Legend of Wyatt Earp came back on TV January 1, 2013 on STARZ/ENCORE Western Channel

DVD sets release dates:
    Boxed Set Season 2   distributed April 30, 2013
    Boxed Set Season 3   to be announced
    Complete Set (226 episodes)   to be announced

For more information about Hugh O'Brian Youth Leadership, go to www.HOBY.org

For Hugh's memorabilia site, go to www.hughobrian.me

Hugh with his "all-star" dad

Hugh with 2nd mom, Leata, whom his dad married after Edith, his mother, passed away

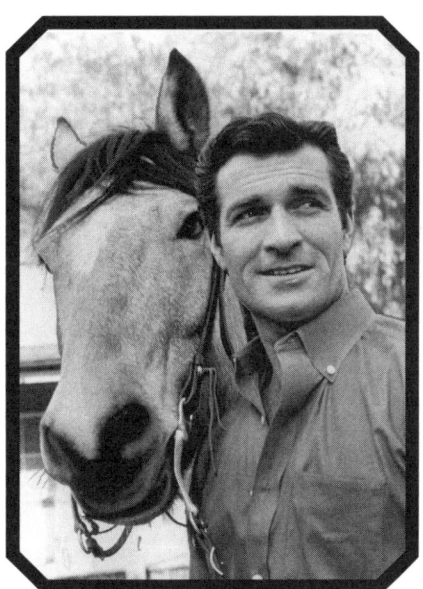

Hugh with animal friends

Hugh shows Ed Sullivan how to do the quick draw on his popular television show

GE True Theatre's Feathertop *starred Hugh as a scarecrow come-to-life. Jane Powell co-starred. 1961*

With Stella Stevens and Tommy Nolan in CBS' General Electric two-hour Movie of the Week, The Graduation Dress, *1960*

Debbie Reynolds shows Hugh how to put on earrings

Hugh with his dear friend George Burns, one of the world's all-time great comedians

Hugh and Virginia all dressed up for a Western-theme party

Hugh with the former queen of Iran, Soraya, whom he dated for several years

With the beautiful Mamie Van Doren

Hugh, in his Wyatt Earp outfit, with (from left), Charlton Heston, Bob Hope, and Jimmy Stewart at a Western event

Visiting old friend Bob Penney at his cabin on the Kenai River in Alaska

Hugh as guest conductor of the Los Angeles Philharmonic Orchestra

Hugh O'Brian Sings released in 1957

Hugh's brother Don with his wife, Jean, and family pet Mickey, Christmas 2013

Hugh, Virginia, and camera-shy KoKo, Christmas 2012

Hugh with assistant Steve Dixon, Christmas 2012

Virginia and Hugh are flanked by their longtime loyal property manager, José Rivera and his family — wife Ellis, daughter Ashannte, José, and son Adonnis

Hugh with longtime friends Howard Lehman (left) and Jim Miller. Above, in the early days. Below, a few years later